MANAGING
BY
STORYING
AROUND

MANAGING
BY
STORYING
AROUND

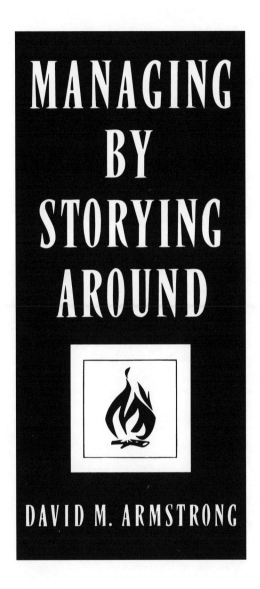

DAVID M. ARMSTRONG

DOUBLEDAY
CURRENCY

New York · London · Toronto · Sydney · Auckland

A CURRENCY BOOK

PUBLISHED BY DOUBLEDAY
a division of Bantam Doubleday Dell Publishing Group, Inc.
666 Fifth Avenue, New York, New York 10103

CURRENCY and DOUBLEDAY are trademarks of Doubleday,
a division of Bantam Doubleday Dell Publishing Group, Inc.

Book design by Debbie Glasserman

Library of Congress Cataloging-in-Publication Data
Armstrong, David M.
    Managing by storying around / David M. Armstrong.
        p.   cm.
    1. Communication in management. 2. Management.
    I. Title.
    HD30.3.A76   1992
    658—dc20   91-26223
                                                  CIP

ISBN 0-385-42154-0

10   9   8   7   6   5   4   3   2   1

First Edition

*This book is dedicated to my wife, Yvonne,
and our sons, Chad and Kurt.
I've been blessed with many wondrous things,
but my family is the
best blessing of all.*

Contents
Stories to Read

Author's note: I've arranged this book so that you can easily find a story that is appropriate for whatever point you are trying to make. For example, if you are looking for stories that will inspire your people to boost company margins, you'd look in "Stories About Finding New Sources of Profit"; stories that deal with empowering your people can be found in "Stories to Inspire Self-management"; and so forth.

Special Acknowledgment

My father, Merrill H. Armstrong, shared with me his thoughts on business; spent countless hours teaching me and nurturing me through my life, and coached me during tough times—not only as a businessman but also as a father. Most of my thoughts on leadership, people, and customers have been developed through my close relationship with my father.

Acknowledgments

To everyone who has supported me, and especially to those about whom these stories were written, I offer my sincere thanks.

I would especially like to thank Paul B. Brown, who helped me clarify my thoughts and suggested some things that helped us run our business better.

And thank you to Harriet Rubin, executive editor of Doubleday/Currency, who saw the potential of this book and believes in storytelling.

Thomas J. Peters helped me understand innovation, showed me how to serve our international customers better, and taught me how to be a better leader.

Introduction
by Tom Peters

This is an enchanting book. And a damned powerful one! It's also one of those slap-yourself-on-the-forehead, "Why didn't I think of that?" books.

There's nothing new about storytelling, of course, as David Armstrong quickly points out. The Greeks did it. Abe Lincoln was a master storyteller. And "Stories Я Us" could have been Ronald Reagan's logo.

Yet there *is* something incredibly new to say about storytelling, which struck me when I first heard David Armstrong talk about his unique approach.

Hey, I'd suggested to execs that they tell stories. But it never occurred to me that you could turn storytelling into a quasi-science, as Armstrong has.

The book is timeless, because storytelling's power is timeless. But it's timely, too. Very timely. The wild and woolly marketplace is demanding that we burn the policy manuals and knock off the incessant memo writing; there's just no time for it. It's also demanding that we empower people—

everyone—to constantly take initiatives. And it turns out that stories are a—if not *the*—leadership answer to both issues.

Policy manuals are no-nos today. But anarchy's not in either. So how do we let people know "what's important around here" without constraining them? The best answer, as I see it—*stories*! Practical stories. Short stories. Stories about their peers. As to empowerment, how do you encourage constant initiative-taking? First, yes, by getting rid of uselessly complex regulations that de facto stomp out initiative-taking. Second, by giving *lots* of examples about "what it means to take an initiative at XYZ Widgets." The answer to "guiding" the imperative initiative-taking process? A good one—*stories*!

David Armstrong limits his mini-heroic tales to a single page. And he admitted to me that getting that one page "right" is agonizing for him. (Writing manuals would be a heck of a lot easier.) But it is a labor of love. And that's a critical point, too.

The book provides seventy-five nifty case examples. The odds are high that you can learn from every one of them. But for heaven's sakes, don't go Xerox them and use them at your place! The "trick," which David mostly hides from you in these pages, is his bone-deep commitment to the process. There's a bit of his soul invested in each one of these small sagas.

That is, storytelling is not for amateurs! Lincoln and Reagan were superb storytellers—because they *believed* in the stories they told. So does David Armstrong.

In the next few pages, Armstrong will lay out his theory. It's a good one, and makes for useful reading. It would be a mistake to skip it. But if you started with this foreword, I would nonetheless suggest that you cheat just a little bit. Go to page 21, and you'll find "The Cafeteria," the first story in the book. It hooked me when I reviewed this manuscript

—*and I'd already seen it before.* The proof is in the pudding. Ahem, the stories themselves.

Read on. Prepare to be charmed. And then backtrack, and think intellectually about the power of the case that's been presented.

MANAGING
BY
STORYING
AROUND

One

A NEW
FORM OF
LEADERSHIP

1

Management by Storytelling?

A quick story about how all this came about, and why management by storytelling can make you a better manager.

Our minister, the Reverend Dr. Dale Kent, was delivering his sermon, and I just didn't understand it—at first.

Dr. Kent was telling the "Talent" story, the one in the Bible, about a man who's about to go on a long trip. Before he leaves, he calls his three servants to his side.

As the first servant comes up, his master gives him five talents—which was a form of currency, like a dollar—and says, "Take care of these talents, good servant, while I am gone." The servant leaves.

The second servant comes up and receives two talents, and his master tells him the same thing. "Take care of these. I'll be back."

The master gives the third servant one talent, and the same message, and then goes off on his trip.

After a long time, the man returns. He calls the servants to his side.

The first servant says, "Master, you delivered to me five talents, and I traded with them, and made another five talents."

"Well done, good and faithful servant . . . I will make you ruler over many things."

The second servant comes up and says, "Master, you delivered to me two talents. Look, I've gained two more talents besides them."

"Well done, good and faithful servant . . . I will make you ruler over many things."

The third servant comes up. He is trembling.

"Master, I knew you to be a hard man, reaping where you have not sown . . . and I was afraid. I hid your talent in the ground." He gives his master the one talent back.

"You wicked and lazy servant . . . You ought to have deposited my money with the bankers, and I would have at least received my talent back with interest." With that, the master "casts the unprofitable servant into the outer darkness."

Now, I'm sitting in church trying to figure out what the servant had done wrong. It wasn't his money to invest. The master said, take care of these talents. He didn't say to invest them. The idea of the third servant going out and hiding the talent sounded pretty good to me. It's what I would have done. So why was he cast into the darkness?

I was confused until Rev. Kent explained the moral of the story: God gives everyone a talent. The ability to run a company, sing a song, write a book, play pro golf. Whatever your talent, God does not expect you to hide it or to conserve it. He expects you to use it to the fullest of your ability.

That made a lot of sense to me. But as I looked around

the church to see if other people agreed with the moral, I noticed something: The people who had been nodding off, or not paying much attention before the sermon began, were now wide awake.

And suddenly I understood an amazing thing. *This happened every Sunday.* People who often attend church probably can recite some of these stories word for word, yet they still listen. People like to hear stories.

What a great way of communicating, I thought. Why can't we do this in our company, Armstrong International Inc.?

Originally what I wanted to do was take the stories in the Bible and apply them to business. I would show how the morals of the Bible's stories applied perfectly to running a company. But the more I thought about it, the more I worried that some people would think I was trying to push religion on them.

I didn't want to do that, but I did want to figure out a way to use storytelling in our company. I loved the idea of telling a story to get a point across. People have always done it. Many of us can remember sitting on our grandfather's knee, listening as he told stories about what it was like "in the good old days." But the tradition predates Grandpa. Native Americans told stories to pass along their culture from one generation to the next, and Jesus was a master storyteller. The fact that his stories are still read today by hundreds of millions of people tells you that storytelling is here to stay.

The reaction to Rev. Kent's sermon showed me that storytelling is just as effective today as it ever was.

Right there in church, I decided we would tell stories in our company. We'd tell stories about our goals and objectives, stories that would explain our core values and our vision of the future, and stories that would celebrate our victories. We'd even share a few stories that would underscore what shouldn't be done.

I started telling stories at Armstrong five years ago, and as I hoped, storytelling has turned out to be an amazingly effective form of communication. Rules, either in policy manuals or on signs, can be inhibiting. But the morals in stories are invariably inviting, fun, and inspiring. Through storytelling, our people can know very clearly what the company believes in, and what needs to be done.

What you'll read in the following pages are some of the stories we have committed to paper over the last few years, stories that have made it easier to manage our thousand employees and help focus everyone on the same goals. Storytelling, as you'll see, is a great way to become a better leader.

2

Why Tell Stories?

I can think of a dozen reasons, right off the bat. Management by storytelling is:

• *Simple.* You don't need an MBA, a college degree, or even a high school diploma to tell stories—or to understand them. You've done it since childhood. Telling stories is just as appropriate for doctors, lawyers, and accountants as it for plumbers, carpenters, and drill press operators.

• *Timeless.* That's another way of saying it's fad-proof. "This, too, shall pass" is a common reaction when the boss starts implementing Management by Objective, or sets up quality circles, or tries to become a One-Minute Manager. Storytelling is ageless.

• *Demographic-proof.* The nature of your work force will change over time, but you'll always be able to use management by storytelling to communicate with them. Telling stories has been, and will continue to be, around forever. Everybody—regardless of age, race, or sex—likes to listen to stories.

• *An excellent way to pass along corporate traditions.* The stories a company tells *shows* what it believes in, and the stories also implicitly instruct people in how they should behave. Is this the kind of office where yelling is expected? Does customer service take precedence over everything else? Through its stories, you get to find out what a company is like.

• *The best form of training I know.* At Armstrong, stories tell people how we do things. They let people know the kinds of things that will get them promoted and what will get them fired.

• *A way to empower people.* The stories lay out guidelines; it is up to the people to get the job done. Once they know what we believe in, they internalize it and, to a very large extent, manage themselves.

• *A wonderful form of recognition.* People love to hear and read about people—especially themselves. Every time an Armstrong employee is mentioned in a story, she receives a framed copy of the original and a personal note from me. You'd be amazed by the number of people who have what they describe as "their story" hanging up in their office or by their machine.

• *A great way to spread the word.* The stories are sent to everyone in the company, so the things we believe in are constantly reinforced. Plus, the stories tell people whom they should see if they have a question. For example, if you read the story about Abe Ghassayi, the head engineer at Armstrong-Hunt in Milton, Florida (page 183), you'll know exactly whom to go to if you have a question about innovation. This is especially helpful to new employees.

• *Fun.* And I don't think the fun part of storytelling can be underestimated. It probably dates back to childhood. We were all told stories as kids and loved to hear them.

"Daddy, tell me a story about the three bears"; "Mommy, tell me again about Cinderella." I'm not a psychologist, but I have to assume that most of us enjoyed our childhood, those carefree days when everything was taken care of for us. If this was true for you, you probably associate hearing stories with good times and having fun.

• *A great recruiting and hiring tool.* When we are interviewing people for a job, they invariably ask what Armstrong International is like. We hand them this storybook. If they read it, they'll know. Also, the stories help us determine if someone will fit in. We often give a story or two (without the morals) to applicants we are thinking about hiring, and ask them to tell us what they think the morals should be. Their answers go a long way toward determining whether we hire them. (See "A Story About Storytelling" on page 243 for an example of how this works.)

• *A great sales tool.* Potential customers want to know what kind of firm they are going to be doing business with if they buy Armstrong International products. This storybook tells them.

• *Memorable.*

In short, storytelling is an effective way to make you a better manager.

3

Leadership by Storying Around

Telling stories changes the way you manage. You become a different kind of leader.

For one thing, you create an environment where people are receptive to change and new ideas. Just think about what happens when you yell at people or order them about. They pull back. They get upset. They withdraw.

But telling stories is friendly and enjoyable. People want to hear what you have to say. They want to know how the story ends. They pay attention.

Also, telling stories forces you, the manager, to pay more attention.

First, you're always looking for a place where a story might fit.

Second, management by storytelling helps you establish an agenda when you are talking with people. We all have a tendency to stop by someone's office, ask "How was your weekend?" and then leave, feeling we have communicated. But if part of your corporate culture involves storytelling, you are bound to go further than that, because you're constantly looking for new material for future stories, and/or trying to find a place where an old story should be told.

Once you have a body of stories, you'll find the need for lots of rules and regulations falls by the wayside. I suppose we could write fifteen or twenty pages covering what the company will reimburse you for when you travel on business, but as you'll see from the "T&E" story on page 81, we have reduced our travel policy to just this: "When you travel for the company, live the way you do at home."

Do you always go to first-class restaurants when you go out to dinner? Then please do that when you're on the road for us. Do you always eat at fast-food places for lunch? Then do that while you are traveling for the company. (Unless, of course, you're meeting with a customer.)

We have found stories to be so effective, they've replaced our policy manual. (Just think of the advantage when you travel, for example. You don't need to lug the policy manual with you to find out what the company will—or won't —pay for.)

Storytelling is a much simpler and more effective way to manage. I don't have to make thousands of individual decisions—is it okay to have a drink with dinner? how about charging an in-room movie to the hotel bill?—about what can or cannot go on someone's T&E report. The story gives people our guidelines, and then it is up to them. Storytelling promotes self-management.

The other nice thing about storytelling is that it helps you spot patterns. Does the same person always seem to be involved when something good (or bad) happens? Stories help you easily identify who should be rewarded and who might need some additional training.

4

How to
Story Around

There are seventy-five stories in this book, and we tell them anytime, anywhere. I've told stories in front of hundreds of our employees at a sales convention, and one-on-one in somebody's office or out in the shop. *When* you tell them is more important than *where*.

We tell stories when we want to make—or underscore—a point. Stories are a great way of getting your message across. People don't like to be lectured.

My great-grandfather, Adam Armstrong, started our company back in 1900 because he wanted to turn his inventions—such as a new way to install bicycle spokes—into products. Today we are an international manufacturing firm with fifteen divisions around the world. (In addition to having offices throughout the United States, we have divisions in Quebec, Belgium, Germany, Singapore, and Japan.)

And just as our company has changed over the last ninety-two years, so has the work force. If there ever was a time when you could just order people to do something, it has long since passed. Telling a story, where you underline the moral, is a great way of explaining to people what needs to be done without saying, "Do this."

Storytelling also provides the continuous reinforcement that management is always striving for. You can say every three months, "Self-control is the best control," or you can send a *different* story every three months that makes the *same* point. Which is going to be more effective? Storytelling, of course.

How do you tell stories? With passion. It's not uncommon for me to act out a story. I'll change the inflection of my voice during the dramatic parts, or do voices if the story involves more than one character. Things like that make stories more effective than lectures.

Before you can teach people something, you have to get them to listen. Stories get them to listen. And including a moral with each story—as we always do—helps ensure they'll understand what they've heard.

When you write a memo, you're never sure it's been read, and even if it has been read, you can't be certain that people understood it. You don't have that problem when you tell stories. You get immediate feedback. Sometimes people will just come out and say, as I did when I heard Rev. Kent tell the "Talent" story, "I don't get it." Sometimes you can tell from their body language. But in either case, you know right away whether you're communicating.

Telling stories is a lot like telling jokes. When you are making a speech, a good opening joke ties in to the subject at hand. The same is true when you tell stories. The story should underscore the point you are trying to make. You'll notice that each story in this book sticks to just one idea. (To make *Managing by Storying Around* easy to use, the stories have been placed into sections that are organized around a specific theme.)

And again like telling a joke, you have to know your audience, and tailor your story accordingly. After all, the whole point of communicating—whether you do it through yelling or through telling stories—is to be heard and understood.

5

Is This Too Far Out?

As you read this, you may think that management by storytelling, or Managing by Storying Around (MBSA) as we call it at Armstrong International, is too far out for you. And quite frankly, you may be right. It *is* different. But there are certain individuals—and I'm one of them—who are not afraid to try something new. Besides, I had some protection just in case this approach to management didn't work. Only one person could fire or demote me. Dad.

So did I really have a lot at risk when I decided to start managing by telling stories? No, nothing, other than my self-esteem and ego.

But to be honest, I didn't see a lot of risk in telling stories. In fact, I saw it as an amazing opportunity. Here was a chance, I thought then—and still believe—to communicate more clearly. It also would be a fun way of explaining our vision of Armstrong International's future.

I found out immediately that this approach to managing would work. The first story I told was the one about ice tea that you'll find on page 115. It got people's attention, and everyone seemed to like it, so at our next meeting I told the

"You Get What You Pay For—or Do You?" story (page 109) and that, too, drew a big response. People started nodding their heads in agreement as I spoke, and they talked about the stories' morals afterward.

And that to me is one of the great appeals of storytelling. *You can underscore the moral,* just as Rev. Kent did when he told the "Talent" story. You'll notice that every story in this book has its moral—or morals—clearly spelled out.

The other thing you should know about these stories is that they are all true. Everything you're about to read actually happened at Armstrong.

Now I know some of the most famous stories are not completely true. The Greek myths, for example, are probably just that, myths. But storytelling *today* has to be based on truth in order to have credibility. If you stretch the truth too far, people are less likely to take the stories—or the morals—seriously. And that means they are less likely to believe—or practice—the points you are trying to make.

Oh, you can fudge a little to emphasize a point. But that's a dangerous thing to do. It's like telling a little white lie—where do you stop? I can think of one or two stories where I might have fudged just a bit, but I really tried to stick to the facts. You have to. At least some of the people hearing the stories are going to know what the facts are. After all, they were there, so you really can't do too much fudging.

You want to stick as close to the truth as you possibly can, and you also want to keep things as simple as you can. You'll notice that each of these stories is short. That's deliberate. No one likes to read long memos or reports. Short stories are friendlier.

Where did all these stories come from? From just about every place in our company. The starting point, though, was almost always a heroic deed. Again, the purpose of these stories is to stress what's important. Showing people going far beyond the call of duty to accomplish what we believe in seemed the easiest way to do that.

When I first started writing these stories, people would come up to me and say things like, "This person stayed a half hour late today, you ought to do a story about that." Or, "That person drove thirty miles out of their way for a customer, you should write about it." For me, those things were pretty routine at our company. I heard those kinds of stories ten times a day. So while I always made it a point to thank the people who made the extra effort, I made it clear to the people suggesting I write a story about them that I needed something more. I wanted something that clearly would show our people, our customers, and even our competitors what Armstrong was all about. That's why I went looking for the heroic. That's what you'll find here.

Management fads come and go, but storytelling has been around forever.

If telling stories has lasted this long, there is probably something to it.

Two

STORIES TO INSPIRE SELF-MANAGEMENT

6

The Cafeteria

At 11:55 A.M. every workday a whistle blows. It's lunch-time. And as you enter the Armstrong cafeteria, nothing—at first—appears out of the ordinary. There are picnic tables, refrigerators filled with sandwiches and soft drinks for sale, coffee machines, microwaves, cigarette and candy machines . . . but wait a minute! The vending machines are un-locked, and there is no cash register. There is no one watching either the food or the money.

The cafeteria is run completely on the honor system. Em-ployees pay for their food or cigarettes by putting their money into an open coin box. On a typical day the box will be filled with well over $100. This system works just fine.

Either you trust your employees or you don't. If you trust
them, you don't need locked cash registers, time clocks,
and scores of supervisors. If you don't trust them,
get rid of them.

The Moral of the Story

• *Self-control is the best control.* And that's true whether we are talking about quality control, work attendance, or paying for food in the cafeteria. We don't have time clocks, yet few people are late for work. We believe in self-inspection, and our scrap rate is 0.2 percent. People don't steal from the concession stand, even though there is unattended cash out in the open. If you give people responsibility for their actions, invariably they'll do the right thing.

• *Think of the message it sends.* By getting rid of locked boxes and needless supervision, you're telling people you believe in them. We've found that faith is rewarded a thousandfold in higher productivity and new ideas.

• *Be open.* Many people feel that withholding information gives them more control, but the opposite is really true. Sharing information with your people gives you more control. Why? Because people impose the control on themselves. For example, we found in one division that people consistently came in under budget when we put them in charge of their department's finances. Once they knew they had the final authority for spending, they didn't buy anything that they didn't absolutely need. They could no longer say, "But my boss said it was okay!"

• *Don't expect quick results.* It will take people a while to get used to having all this control over their work lives, so start small. Maybe remove the time clock one month, open some locked doors the next. Eventually, by observing how their leaders treat them, they'll truly believe that they have control.

7

The Time Clock

We had just acquired Everlasting Valve, a union shop with a traditional type of labor-management relationship, and our managers wanted to show the employees how *we* did things. Without consulting anyone at Corporate, the managers decided to remove the time clock. "If we really believe our people are our strongest asset, then we should treat them as if they are," the managers said to themselves. "Why should we have a time clock that humiliates them? They're adults. They know what time they are supposed to be at work. They know what's expected of them."

The managers went into the shop and took down the clock. Talk has always been cheap, but here was a group of leaders who, through their actions, were making it clear to their people that they believed the people they worked with were important and trustworthy.

How did the union employees react? They were shocked. At first, they expected the time clock would be used as a negotiating tool during the upcoming contract talks. But the fact that management wanted nothing in return proved to them that they really were trusted.

They've proved they're worthy of that trust. We haven't had a problem with people coming in late. In fact, some people are now coming in early.

People know what time it is. If they don't, a time clock won't get them to work on time.

The Moral of the Story

• *Do the right thing—willingly.* Don't turn issues of respect—eliminating the time clock, unlocking closed doors—into bargaining issues. Do what's right. It will work. People still came to work on time and gave us a full day's work, even without having to punch in or out.

• *Time ticks on.* Your people know what time it is. If they don't, no time clock is going to help get them to work on time, or convince them to give you an honest day's work.

• *Delegate.* It was the people on the front line who had the responsibility for making sure the Everlasting division was productive, so it just made sense for them to handle the time-clock issue as they saw fit.

• *Listen.* The leaders at Everlasting had heard their people complain about the time clock. It symbolized they were not trusted. Not only did the leaders listen to the message, they took action.

• *Treat people like people.* Life is easier, and you are more productive in the long term, if you show respect for the people who work for you. A "do it or else" attitude works only in the short term.

8

Production Bonus

The year was 1907, or 1908, nobody remembers for sure. But what they do remember was that it was common eighty-five years ago for people to take the day off and go hunting or fishing to help put food on the table.

Back then Armstrong Machine Works employed about a dozen people, and a missing employee, or two, could ruin the production schedule.

People kept telling Adam Armstrong, my great-grandfather and the founder of what is now Armstrong International, that he'd have to hire more people, but Great-grandad didn't see it that way. "Why don't we offer our employees an attendance bonus instead?" he asked.

"How can we afford to give a bonus?" his sales manager said.

"It would be a lot cheaper than hiring new employees," Adam replied.

He was right. The attendance bonus took care of the company's absenteeism problems. Over time—as fewer and fewer people hunted for food—the attendance bonus evolved into the production bonus we use to this day.

It is paid on two very simple measurements: (1) The more product shipped, the bigger the bonus, and (2) the smaller the number of people required to produce those orders, the bigger the bonus.

Everybody—secretaries, managers, office personnel—is counted when we are calculating how long it takes to produce a product, and everybody, including our division heads, receives exactly the same bonus. This creates team spirit.

We calculate the bonus once a month, post it everywhere, and you get a *separate* bonus check with your next paycheck.

Everybody can tell you how much the bonus was last month. More importantly, everyone can tell you what we have to do to increase it.

"What gets measured gets done."

TOM PETERS

The Moral of the Story

• *Here today, here tomorrow.* Most motivational techniques change from year to year. We've been paying a production bonus since the 1930s. Why? Because it works. People are rewarded for their performance. The harder they work, and the more orders they ship, the bigger their bonus.

• *Motivational systems must be simple.* And clear. If we ship more products, or we do the same amount of work with fewer people, the bigger the bonus. This is simple to understand. It also allows people to work toward the same goal.

• *Motivational systems need to be fair.* Paying for performance is fair to the employee—and the company. Anything fair has a good chance of working—and surviving. In determining how the bonus is to be paid, you must determine if you want to give it when people are out sick, on maternity leave, or on jury duty. For example, we pay the bonus even when a person is out on vacation. Why? Because everyone knows the bonus is higher in some months than in others—it all depends on the seasonality of our products—and if we didn't pay bonuses during vacations, everyone would want to take vacation during poor bonus months.

• *Motivational systems need to support your business philosophy.* If quality is important to you, your bonus system must underscore that point. In our case, each part returned because of quality problems reduces the bonus.

• *Pay frequently.* Handing out the bonus once a month works far better than paying it once a year. It continually reinforces what's important, and people can see almost immediately the relationship between hard work and high pay.

• *Pay everybody.* All level of employees, from the lowest to the very highest, receive the same bonus. If the guy on the line gets $160 for the month, the head of production does, too. Everybody should win—and lose—together, thus promoting team spirit.

9

Sick Days

Last week as I was walking through the shop, I bumped into Bill C. Hartman, foreman in the punch press department. I asked—as I always do—whether he had any stories I could write up.

"Sorry, David, I don't. But as long as you're here, I have a question about our sick leave policy. I was told we only get 75 percent of our unused sick leave when we retire. Is that right? I have 480 hours, or sixty days coming, cutting it to forty-five days doesn't sound quite fair to me."

"Bill, there were two reasons we created our sick leave policy—which pays you for not being sick—about fifteen years ago. First, it was a way of thanking our employees who always—despite rain, snow, gloom of night, or just general aches and pains—come to work. The second reason was more selfish. Like those of many companies with plants in the upper Midwest, many of our employees seem to come down with a cold or flu on the opening day of deer (or trout) season. (People may no longer hunt to put food on the table, but they still seem to enjoy it.) To boost attendance on those days, and reward people who always come to work, we created this policy.

"I think it is a pretty good policy. Here's how it works. At our largest divisions, all employees are entitled to forty hours (five days) of paid sick leave a year." (In your first and last year you receive eight hours for every three months you've worked.)

"If you don't use all your sick days in a given year, you can carry them over—indefinitely. That gives you a chance to make a lot of money. At retirement, or when you leave Armstrong, you'll be paid 75 percent of your hourly wage for each day of sick leave you've accumulated, providing you've been with the company at least five consecutive years.

"A simple example will make this clear. Say you have a hundred sick days coming to you when you retire. We will pay you the equivalent of seventy-five days' (that's fifteen weeks') salary—based on your *current* wage, no matter what you were earning when you accumulated the sick day.

"So you see, Bill, you get 75 percent of your *future* wages."

"That's a lot fairer than what I thought," Bill said. "Thanks for explaining it to me."

"No, thank you, Bill," I said reaching for my pen. "I have another story."

Just because an idea is old does not mean that it's outdated.

The Moral of the Story

• *If it's important, measure it, and pay for it.* If good service and quality are high priorities, then a reliable work force is essential. That's why we reward good attendance.

• *The glass is half full.* We don't track the number of jobs done wrong, only the ones done right. We don't tell you how many days you were out sick, we tell you the balance in your "sick day account." We want to show people what they are doing right, not tell them what they are doing wrong.

• *Adam Armstrong's ideas are still going strong . . . some eighty-five years later.* Remember the "attendance bonus" in the last story? Remember why it was started? Our sick leave policy sounds similar, doesn't it? We are constantly looking for ways to update old ideas.

• *Be careful what you wish for, it might come true.* Our sick day program works, but it's expensive. Equally important, it's now part of our culture. It would be very difficult to stop. Before you start a program, think it through. Ask yourself: Is this something we are committed to long-term?

• *Ownership is essential for any program to work.* One key factor in the success of our sick day policy is that the workers understand it and believe in it. Our office staff was given the option of adopting the same policy, but voted it down. For whatever reason, it wasn't right for them. If we had tried to force it on them, I am sure that it would have failed.

10

The Blue-Tag Special

Some twenty years ago, we found a wonderful way of improving quality. We cut back on the number of inspectors. Our scrap rate has been substantially below the industry norm ever since.

Yes, there is still a quality assurance department. But it only has three members now, down from eight, and its primary job is to resolve major quality problems. Our QA people only do occasional spot-checks.

So who is making sure that things are running right?

Our machine operators.

What we've told them is, "You're responsible for the quality of the parts you produce." And as my last visit to Armstrong Machine Works showed, the program is working just fine.

As I walked through the shop, I noticed six big trays, containing five hundred castings each, that were marked with blue tags. The tags are the symbol a machine operator uses when he feels there is a problem with the part he has just worked on.

Placing tags on those products was no small decision.

First, it meant the machine operator—on his own—shut down production to flag the problem. (After examining some of the castings he had produced, the operator had decided that the entire batch was probably bad.)

Second, we are talking about a lot of money here. Those three thousand castings represented thousands of dollars' worth of parts that were not going to be shipped until the machine operator and the QA person were satisfied that they were okay.

And this is exactly the way it is supposed to be. "Quality is very important" is one of the first things people are told when they're hired at Armstrong. "Nobody will be disciplined for trying to improve quality. On the other hand, if someone allows or hides bad quality, he will be in serious trouble."

The machine operators have taken this message seriously, and our quality has improved ever since.

If you know someone is going to double-check your work, you may not check it yourself. If you want to lower costs and improve quality, reduce the number of inspectors you have. Make each person responsible for his own work.

The Moral of the Story

• *Less inspectors means more inspections.* By reducing the number of inspectors we have, we have actually increased the number of inspections we do. We now have 150 people (the machine operators) checking quality, instead of eight people in Quality Assurance.

• *Don't just fix the problem, fix the system.* There are two keys to making self-inspection work. First, fix the problem. In this case, we found the castings were flawed. The machine operator attached the blue tag to the castings, and on the back described the problem and the batch number in which it occurred. But fixing the problem is not enough. Problems will happen over and over again until we fix the system that allowed them to occur. Here, we needed to find out how we ended up with defective castings in the first case.

• *If people believe in a program, they'll do a better job.* Our machine operators *know* they can stop production and flag a problem, and they feel comfortable doing it. They know that decision won't cost them their jobs. It is their job. How do they know this? We've told them, for one thing. More important, it takes one brave soul to get the ball rolling. Once people see that management praises him for trying to improve quality—instead of yelling at him for stopping production—they will believe the company is serious about improving quality.

Three

STORIES TO MAKE PEOPLE BRAVE AND WISE

11

Leaders Make Mistakes, Too

Armstrong-Hunt in Milton, Florida, had received an order for copper coils that we knew would be tricky to produce. The work required intricate welding, and after we were finished it was clear the job was not up to our standards. We were certain that it was just a matter of time before the welds would crack.

Chuck Rockwell, the general foreman, knew there were two possible solutions. We could scrap the coils and start over. That would cost us about $2,000 in material alone, and you'd have to add our labor costs on top of that. Our second option was to grind away the bad welds and try to salvage the job. Because Chuck had to pick me up at the airport, he left the decision up to his foreman.

By the time Chuck and I got to the plant, the foreman and his welders had decided to scrap the product and start over.

"It's my fault we had this problem," Chuck told me in front of his staff. "I knew from past experience that welding copper is extremely difficult, but I didn't spend enough time with either our foreman or our welders to show them what needed to be done."

Chuck estimated that we could recover about $300 if the coils were sold for scrap. He decided to take the $300 and throw a party to celebrate his mistake because he was certain people would learn from it. From this day forward, he knew, we wouldn't undertake a new job until *everyone* understood what needed to be done. They would also learn that *everyone* makes mistakes, even the boss.

I am very proud of what Chuck did—for two reasons. In front of his coworkers and his boss (me), he took the responsibility for making a mistake. And he decided to celebrate it. Here's an outstanding example of a leader who led by example. He said *publicly* it's okay to fail.

You have to be brave enough to fail as a leader.

—OLLE BOVAN, HEWLETT PACKARD

The Moral of the Story

• *Celebrate your mistakes—publicly.* Seeing is believing. People will come up with more ideas when their leaders demonstrate *by their actions* that they will support failure, especially when something is learned from it, as it was in Chuck's case. If the boss can admit failure, then the troops feel more comfortable trying new ventures. How can the boss get upset if a good idea fails? After all, he's failed, too.

• *Supporting failure does not mean supporting (or even tolerating) sloppiness.* The only time failure is good is when

(a) something is learned from it, and (b) the idea is quickly modified.

• *To fail is not enough.* You must fail big. Tom Peters said that, and he's right. Significant gains come from significant risks.

12

The $5 Thank-you

How do you say thank you, when a mere thank-you is not enough? My solution involved creative swiping.

I had read a story about a CEO who was just blown away one day by something wonderful an employee had done. He wanted to honor the guy immediately, but he had nothing to give him. So the CEO reached out across the table, where there was a bowl of fruit, and pulled out a banana. He gave the employee the banana as a token of his appreciation. Well, the idea caught on, and the company created a banana stickpin, made out of gold, that became a major award to win at the company.

I loved the story, but I wondered what you could do if you didn't have a banana lying about. I began wondering what you also had a chance of handing out, and it hit me. Money. I started carrying a bunch of $5 bills, which I hand out when someone has done something extraordinary.

I had thought about giving out $100 bills, but realized that could cause some problems. If I gave out hundreds, there was bound to be jealousy or resentment. People were going to come up to me and say, "Why did he get a $100 bill for what he did, when I did this and it was so much better?" However, no one is going to say anything about someone receiving $5, because it's not that much money. But it is recognition, which I think is important, and it is money, which I also think is important.

Like everyone else, we give out plaques and have recognition dinners, but there is something about money—even if it is a small amount of money—that people really like. Five dollars offers recognition and allows the recipient to buy herself lunch on us—but it isn't a large enough amount to cause resentment. No one has ever complained. And nobody has ever turned down the $5. Everybody likes the recognition. And the free lunch.

Don't spoil praise by breeding resentment.

The Moral of the Story

• *Catch people doing something right.* And reward them. Immediately. As the $5 shows, the reward doesn't have to be anything big.

• *Celebrate the small wins, too.* You already make a big deal about major victories, but don't forget to cheer for the little things—like the person who stays late to get a memo done, or who makes that one extra phone call.

• *Be consistent.* For a small victory, everyone—from a janitor to the executive vice president—gets $5. It's another way of saying that *everyone's* ideas are equally important.

13

Be Yourself, But . . .

It happened again the other day. I was on a plane and ran into a competitor—although it could have been a supplier, or anyone else we do business with—wearing clothes that were probably best suited for cleaning out the garage. The first words out of his mouth were, "Oh, I am so embarrassed about the way I'm dressed."

I wonder why he dressed that way in the first place.

I always dress up when I travel, because you never know whom you will run into, and rightly or wrongly, people judge you in part by what you are wearing.

And if they are judging you, they are also subtly judging the company you work for.

In westerns, you know within seconds who the
good guys are. They wear white hats.
In the business world, people judge you almost as quickly
based on what you are wearing. Perhaps it isn't fair, but
it's reality.

The Moral of the Story

• *Mirror, mirror . . .* We don't have a dress code at Armstrong. We tell people to be themselves. But we also tell them the way they dress is a reflection of our company.

• *Every impression is important.* The way you dress is just one of the things you—and your company—will be judged on. How you talk, how you answer a letter or phone, and even your manners will tell customers if you're worthy of their business. Perhaps perceptions based on these intangibles aren't fair, but that's the way it is.

• *What do your clothes say about you?* Do they tell the world you are a banker, a lawyer, an artist, or an executive? Or are they undermining your position?

• *Be prepared.* The airline loses your luggage, someone picks you up at the airport and takes you directly to an unscheduled meeting, or maybe you run into a potential customer. These are all excellent reasons for you to "dress for success" when you travel. If you're dressed up, you don't need to worry about surprises.

Four

STORIES
ABOUT
CORE
VALUES

14

Lead Us Not into Temptation

On a cold Sunday morning, the Reverend Dr. Dale Kent told our congregation a story with such passion, that I want to share it with you. It has a great deal of meaning for me.

. . .

"My first day at college brought me face-to-face with my roommate, who happened to be a Native American. As we talked, he told me a story about a Native American boy who was entering manhood.

"To prove he was worthy of joining the rest of the men in his village, the young man decided to climb to the peak of a very high mountain. He put on a deerskin shirt, covered himself with a blanket, and started his journey.

"After a great climb, he finally reached the top, and as he looked out he said, 'I can see the whole world.'

"Just then, he heard a noise below his feet. He looked down and saw a rattlesnake. The boy was just about to jump back when the snake said, 'Please, don't leave. I'm very cold, and there's no food to eat. Please put me under your shirt and take me down the mountain.'

" 'I can't,' said the boy. 'I know what you are. You're a rattlesnake. You'll bite me and I'll die.'

" 'No, I promise,' said the snake. 'Please take me where I may live in warmth and find food to eat.'

"The boy, with goodness in his heart, decided to take pity on the rattlesnake. He put the snake under his shirt and headed down the mountain.

"When he reached the valley, he placed the snake on the ground. As he did, the snake struck, biting the boy on the wrist.

" '*You promised,*' said the boy just before he died. 'Why did you bite me?'

" 'You knew what I was,' said the snake. 'You knew what you were doing.' "

You don't lie, cheat, or steal off the job. Why would you do it at work?

The Moral of the Story

• *Don't check your sense of right and wrong at the door.* Morality exists twenty-four hours a day. We deal with temptation every day—just consider what happens at work. We might be tempted to steal product from the factory, or steal time, or falsify an expense voucher, or take office supplies home. We are constantly tempted, as the boy was.

• *Temptation is everywhere.* Especially at work, where you might try to justify your actions by saying, "The company can afford what I'm taking." Be careful not to fall into temptation's evil grasp. Once you start doing something you shouldn't, it is difficult to stop.

• *Ask, and ye shall receive.* If you need a loan, or tools to perform a task at home, just ask, and you'll probably receive assistance from your coworkers or company. There's no need to take what you will be probably be given anyway.

15

Our Promise
to Fred Kemp

If an efficiency expert took a look at the layout of our screw machine and punch press division, he'd have a cow. The parts move from one end of our property to the other and back again, in no logical order. All that travel means higher labor costs and lower productivity.

And I couldn't be prouder. Why? Well, the story really begins back in 1972.

Back then it was clear that we'd need a new building to house our expanding screw machine and punch press departments. After much study and evaluation, we designed an addition that would keep the moving of unfinished goods to a minimum. The new building would be located right next to our old one.

The layout was as efficient as could be. There was only one problem with the plan. It would require us to put the new building right where there was a home. The house belonged to Fred Kemp, then in his mid-seventies, who was a retired Armstrong employee.

The solution seemed simple. We'd buy Fred's house, tear

it down, and build the new plant next to the existing manufacturing plant.

When we looked into the situation further, we found that we wouldn't even have to buy the house. We already owned it. The building committee went to the company president, Howard Lambentson, for permission to begin demolition.

The president vetoed the plan.

"Fred has lived in the house forever," he said. "His children grew up there, and it really is the only place he's ever called home. I know he loves that place. We bought it from him years ago, when it looked like we'd have to expand onto his property someday. But when we bought it, I promised he could stay there as long as he liked. Making him move now might upset him to the point where it shortens his life. We'll build the new plant on the other side of the property."

This is one of the few times I am proud we are inefficient.

You can't put a price tag on integrity. You must *always* do the right thing *no matter what it costs.*

The Moral of the Story

• *Live the message.* Armstrong's management says constantly that it values its employees and former employees. Building the new plant on the other side of the property showed there isn't any doubt.

• *Show respect—to everyone.* Respect is caring and trust. A retiree deserves this respect as much as an employee, customer, or vendor.

• *You'll be paid back.* When Fred sold us his house, he really could have taken advantage of us. He knew we'd need his property someday, and could have demanded an extremely high price. He sold it to us at market value. If you take care of your people, your people will take care of you.

16

The Cocktail Bomb

One day a factory worker spilled some cleaning alcohol on the floor in our Computrol plant. That represented a major problem. Computrol manufactures bottom-line fish finders and other electronic components, and it's very important to keep an electronics plant free of dirt, dust, static electricity, or liquids. Any contaminant can cause the products to malfunction.

The question was how would he clean up the mess. With rags? Paper towels? A mop?

The worker's solution was simple. He set the alcohol on fire and burned it clean. Even though he was one of our better employees, he was fired on the spot. He had broken a core value: safety.

Nobody is above the law. *Nobody.* If someone clearly breaks one of your company's core values, he must be fired immediately.

The Moral of the Story

• *It's either important or it's not.* Core values must be practiced and enforced. This was not a safe way of cleaning up the cleaning solvent. In fact, it was extremely dangerous. Nobody likes to fire people, but it was called for here.

• *Managing by example sometimes means you have to reinforce a negative example.* Here is one of the few times that we made a big deal about somebody doing something wrong. The potential consequences of setting the alcohol on fire made it too important not to.

• *Don't wait.* If someone violates a core value, take action immediately. Any hesitation or delay will cause people to think, "Maybe this value wasn't such a big deal in the first place."

17

The $125,000
Thank-you

All companies go through tough times, and Armstrong, unfortunately, is no exception. In 1987, for the first time since the Depression, we put a wage freeze into effect to help us get through what looked like it would be a very difficult year.

Our employees were amazing. They accepted the freeze with very few complaints. "The company has always been fair with me" seemed to be the prevailing attitude. "Now it's my turn to be fair to the company."

A few months into the new year, it looked like 1987 was going to be much better than projected. We decided that not only could we give everybody raises, but we could afford to make them retroactive. The back pay came to about $400 per employee.

We didn't give our employees that $400 by check. Instead, we called everybody into the recreation building where my father, company president, was standing behind a large table covered with a white sheet. He explained that since Armstrong was doing better than anticipated, the company wanted to share its good fortune.

With that, he lifted the sheet, and everyone saw that the table was covered with $10 bills—some 12,500 of them—stacked two feet high.

One by one, each employee came up, shook my dad's hand and those of the company's managers, and was told, "Thank you for your understanding." They walked away with forty crisp, new $10 bills.

If there's a point to be made, either good or bad, do it dramatically. People will remember.

The Moral of the Story

• *Integrity is a two-way street.* Both sides showed integrity here. The employees took the wage freeze with few complaints. They wanted to help their company. But the company demonstrated integrity, too. It didn't have to make the raises retroactive. It could have kept the $125,000, and nobody would have been the wiser.

• *Thank-yous must be sincere.* We wanted to let our employees know we really appreciated their actions. Sure, we could have given everybody a check, but it wouldn't have had the same effect.

• *Messages with a smile.* There is nothing wrong with a little fun. Seeing $125,000 up close is dramatic, entertaining —and when part of that pile of bills is yours—definitely fun.

18

Surprise! There Are Twenty-four Hours in the Day

It looked as if we were going to have to spend a lot of money.

To meet customer demand, we had decided to redesign our water heater. But because we run as efficiently as we possibly can, I found as I walked around our plant that we didn't have anyone we could spare to do the work. We'd have to hire additional engineers and machinists, and buy more equipment.

But Les Newbre, night foreman, proved that wasn't necessarily true. "David, the same machinery we used full-time during the day could be used to build the water heater at night," he said. Les reminded me we even had people available at night who could work on the proto-type.

What we had here was an extra eight hours—and in the case of our other plants that run twenty-four hours a day, an extra sixteen hours—for design and manufacturing. Les Newbrie was the very first person I've ever heard suggest that the night shift help *create* a new product. We had a huge hidden resource, he explained—our second and third shifts—that we could use.

The key to taking advantage of this resource was better communication. For example, now we have the foremen on the day and night shifts meet for a half hour each day to discuss what has been done, what needs to be done, and how each shift can help the other. All our engineers, sales managers, and product managers leave their home numbers so they can be contacted at night.

If becoming more competitive today is our goal, we must find—and use—every hidden resource that we have.

Almost anything that can be done during the day can be done at night, yet we tend to operate as if the world comes to a stop at 5 P.M.

The Moral of the Story

• *Why are meetings always held during the day?* Les, like many other people on the night shift, wanted to be part of the company, but we—unintentionally—were making it hard for him by scheduling most meetings during the day. That wasn't fair to him.

• *Out of sight, out of mind?* When was the last time you spent any time with the people who work the second or third shift? Did you meet them when it was the middle of the day *for them?*

• *Free time for the taking?* Can you afford to compete with two thirds of your assets lying dormant? That's exactly what you're doing if the focus of your business is eight to five. Even if you run a "traditional" service company that only operates during the day, there are still ways to use your assets at night. For example, you can let a telemarketing firm use your phones, or a typing service rent your word processors.

Five

STORIES ABOUT HEROIC PEOPLE

19

F-L-O-W-E-R-S
Spells Pride

During my most recent visit to Everlasting Valve, I noticed newly planted flowers blooming just outside the front door. I mentioned how nice I thought that looked. One of our managers told me that about a month before Fritz Kolzar, who worked in shipping-receiving, had come in on a Saturday to plant them. Fritz had told his colleagues that he wanted the place to look good.

It did. I was completely amazed that somebody would come in on his own time to plant flowers on company grounds. Not only was this done on a Saturday, but it was done by a union employee, at a place where management and the union had differing ideas over job responsibility. (I'm sure that neither management nor the union ever considered planting flowers as part of a job description.)

As I thought about it, I realized that management knew exactly who had planted the flowers, and that it was happy to have Fritz recognized. I also realized that the union had not given Fritz a hard time about doing something beyond the call of duty. Many unions would have. To me, the simple act of planting flowers showed how union and management can function together if they treat each other with respect.

I am honored to be able to share this story with our other divisions, and I want to offer my sincere thanks to everyone at Everlasting, the union, and especially Fritz Kolzar.

Caring is contagious.

The Moral of the Story

• *The Golden Rule works in reverse, too.* If you treat people the way you'd like to be treated, odds are they will treat you the same way. We showed the union respect by taking out the time clock, and the next thing we knew a union employee was coming in on his own time to plant flowers to make sure the building looked nice.

• *A machine would never plant flowers.* We know more and more companies are becoming automated. They want to reduce the number of employees, and thereby reduce costs. But something is lost in the process. Machines don't care, they don't make the extra effort. A machine would never plant flowers. Only people like Fritz Kolzar care.

• *Like the longest journey, the road to change starts with but a single step.* Change is always difficult, especially when you're dealing with two groups—like labor and management—with different points of view. We can hope that Fritz' small step, like our decision to pull out the time clock, will help get us to the point where both union and management *constantly* work together.

20

Thanksgiving Day

Thanksgiving Day is a time for rest, family, and a big turkey dinner. No one at the office, or in the plant, works at Armstrong on this holiday. Nobody, that is, except Ed Kirchner and Larry Haag. They worked last Thanksgiving.

Armstrong Machine Works (AMW) had recently installed a flexible machining center, a huge machine that is capable of producing dozens of finished castings an hour. The major advantage of this machine is that it can run unmanned seven days a week, twenty-four hours a day. It does that day in and day out, except when it breaks down. Thanksgiving Day it broke down.

Larry Haag, machine operator, called Ed Kirchner, who is in charge of maintaining the machine, and the two of them spent five hours getting it back up and running. The next day, which was also a holiday for us, Larry stopped by just to make sure everything was still okay. It wasn't. The machine was down again. Once again he called Ed. Two hours later, the machine was going full speed. It ran the rest of the weekend without a problem.

The commitment Larry and Ed showed is typical at Armstrong. For example, this same machine needs to be loaded with castings every six to eight hours. And if you want it to run seven days a week—which we do, so we can get orders to our customers faster—that means somebody must work weekends to keep the machine filled.

We explained the problem to the employees at AMW, and even before we could ask for volunteers, several people stepped forward and offered to work weekends. We owe our thanks to Mark Henline, John Henline, Brad Kinney, Keith Pratt—and once again to Larry Haag and Ed Kirchner. Because of them, the machine has been operating on weekends the last two years, allowing us to serve our customers better.

Procrastination is the kiss of death.

The Moral of the Story

• *Either you are committed or you ain't.* We believe in service, but sometimes service is only possible with real commitment. Larry Haag and Ed Kirchner showed they are committed, even on holidays.

• *Machinery is not a company's strongest asset.* People are. Our expensive machining center would be worthless without people like Larry and Ed to keep it running. The machine would not have fixed itself, and started running again, without their commitment.

• *Commitment is not enough.* The desire to help is fine, but you also have to know what to do. Ed had been trained by the machine's manufacturer, Giddings & Lewis, to fix the machine. The manufacturer had also trained Larry to not only run the machine, but also to be able to repair its programming if anything went wrong. That knowledge, plus their commitment, made it possible to get the machine running again.

• *Once you lose a day,* you can never get it back. If Larry and Ed had not worked on Thanksgiving, we would have lost four days of production (the Thursday of Thanksgiving, Friday, which was also a holiday, and the weekend). Once that time is gone, it can never be replaced.

21

'Twas the Night Before Christmas

As the clock approaches the appointed time for the company Christmas party, the phone rings in the sales department.

"Hello, Walt Deacon speaking."

"Walt, this is Bill Finnie [a salesman] at Power Specialties. We have an emergency. An IBM vice president says he *must* have nine humidifiers shipped to him by the end of the day. He said he'd pay anything—air freight, overtime, whatever it takes—but he needs them to ship today. Can you do it?"

"Let me check with Ken Handy. I'll get right back to you."

The phone rings in the production department.

"Ken, this is Walt. What are the chances of shipping nine humidifiers today?"

Ken looked up the number of humidifier bodies on the inventory report, and saw he had only five on hand.

"Would the customer take a partial order?" he asked. "Wait a second before you answer that. Let me check with the shop."

Ken called Walt back a few minutes later.

"I found enough bodies," Ken said. "We can ship nine humidifiers, if you can find someone to assemble them."

Walt calls Jerry Henry, who is in charge of all the shop foremen.

"Jerry? Walt. Can we assemble nine humidifiers and ship them today?"

"I'm not sure," Jerry said. "Let me check with Bill Mc-Clain [foreman in the humidifier department]."

Bill McClain called back and said he and Elwood "Sag" Kinney could get the work done.

"Walt? This is Jerry. Tell your customer that we *can* ship today."

Walt called Bill Finnie back.

"Bill, you're a Christmas Scrooge. The company Christmas party starts in a few minutes, but yes, we'll be able to ship your order." Walt then went on to explain what it was going to take to get the order out by the end of the day.

"Bill, I think you should buy some beer and send it to the attention of Jerry Henry to show your appreciation."

"Walt, could you buy the beer, and I'll pay you back?" Bill asked.

"No, sometimes you salesmen forget what kind of effort it takes to get an emergency order out the door. I want you to buy some beer that you can get only in Boston and send it to Jerry Henry, who will distribute it."

I know he did, because as I write this I am looking at a bottle cap that says "Samuel Adams" on it.

No pain? No gain. The only way I know to hold on to customers, and gain new ones, is through pain—the pain, sweat, and commitment your people give to satisfying the customer.

The Moral of the Story

• *Recognition must be sincere.* Too many times, managers and vendors ask for the extraordinary without realizing what's required. Make the extra effort—like searching out a local beer—to say thanks for someone who has gone out of his way for you.

• *Recognition must come from the right person.* Walt Deacon could have thanked his people—and he did—but it was important that Bill Finnie, the person making the extraordinary request, also acknowledge the effort it took to ship those nine humidifiers.

• *We did not bill IBM for overtime.* IBM is a good customer. Why should we take advantage of a good customer? We would *not* have billed a first-time customer for all this extra effort, in the hope it would lead to future orders, so there is no reason to bill a lifelong customer like IBM. (We hope this gives them another reason to stick with us.) The real payoff for all this extra effort comes in the form of *future* business we'll receive.

Six

STORIES TO KICK-START URGENCY

22

√

The new week began as people arrived at work. As they approached their work stations, each noticed a calendar strategically located where it would be seen. On the calendar was a blue check mark with no explanation. Curiosity set in.

The next week, posters arrived in the plant with a blue check mark—creating yet more curiosity. Soon, people found coffee mugs, hats, scratch pads, parking places, and other items with blue check marks on them. This was a mystery which had to be solved. Finally, they were told what the blue check mark stood for—"Consider It Done." This is the new vision statement for Armstrong and its divisions. The blue check mark is a symbol which we use to "check off" items on a list of things to do.

The new vision statement promotes a sense of urgency in every decision we make. Since this philosophy of urgency had been promoted for the last two years through the old vision statement, "Armstrong—Expect a Difference Now," it was essential to build excitement and interest in the new vision statement. It was, therefore, critical to use curiosity and mystery to promote it.

Today, the tortoise would lose the race to the hare.

The Moral of the Story

• *Remember the childhood story about the race between the tortoise and the hare?* The moral was: Slow, but steady, wins the race. But today you cannot just be slow and steady, because too many competitors (hares) are moving fast and they are no longer likely to fall asleep.

• *"Consider It Done" means:* Whatever you are working on, do it *quickly* and stay within the boundaries of our core values. When you're faced with a question of what to do, the answer will come easier if you remember you are to practice urgency.

• *"Consider It Done" is for everyone.* Clearly, the success of our vision will depend upon everyone practicing urgency. There can be no exceptions.

• *"Consider It Done" can work for every division.* Your division may have its own strategy or business plan that promotes service, quality, innovation, etc. Our vision should be applied to your division's strategy. If your division is focusing on quality, it should do so quickly.

• *Like stories, urgency is here to stay.* Our society and technology are changing rapidly. In the past, product improvements took years; today, they take months; tomorrow they will take days. Today's emphasis on quality, service, innovation, diversification, acquisition, leveraged buyout or whatever will pass with other fads. Urgency, on the other hand, will always be needed to stay ahead of the competition. Our vision can last forever.

• *Ask yourself, do my actions promote urgency?* "Consider it done" is the answer you give if somebody asks, "Did that order ship?" "Can you finish the lab test?" "When will you fix the machine?" "Will you return a call to this customer?" If you answer, "Consider it done," you'll have to do it.

23

The Salesman Who Quit Selling

One day Marv Middleton, manager of the Armstrong Machine Works' manufacturing engineers, and a tool salesman were walking through the machining department while the salesman made his pitch.

"Marv, I tell you these carbide cutters are the greatest thing on the market. They'll cut six times faster than any tool you have."

Rich Wright, a machine operator, overheard the salesman and asked a question.

"Sir, do you happen to have any of those cutters with you?"

"I sure do," the salesman replied.

"Well, why don't you get a couple and we'll find a jig and put them to the test right now?"

The salesman went out to his car, brought back the carbide cutters, and gave them to Rich. He installed them and went to work. Within ten minutes, Rich had broken two of the carbide cutters that were supposed to last, in the words of the salesman, "almost forever." Rich handed the remaining cutters back to the salesman.

"Sir, thank you, but what we have seems to be performing better," Rich said, and he headed back to his machine.

The salesman put his head down and mumbled a thank-you to Marv. "I'll be back in the future with a better product."

Nike is right: Just do it.

The Moral of the Story

• *Stop talking; start doing.* Marv could have spent a great deal of time talking with the salesman. But sometimes we talk too much. There's only one sure way to determine if something will work—try it! The fact that Rich persuaded the salesman to install a unit and test it saved us a great deal of time and money.

• *If you are going to "just do it,"* do it now. Try the idea immediately. Don't wait a week or two to develop support documents and CYA memos.

• *Involve everyone who might be affected by your decision.* Here's a case where the machinist, Rich, who would use the cutting tool, got involved. He was able to determine very quickly whether or not the new product had any merit.

• *Things get done quickly* . . . when people are comfortable around each other. Because Rich is comfortable around Marv, he could interrupt, and expedite a decision about the carbide cutters.

Seven

STORIES THAT MAKE OUR POLICY MANUAL OBSOLETE

24

T&E

An old friend, Charlie Scott, financial controller at Computrol, called looking for some help. He had been told to establish travel and entertainment guidelines for his division, and he wanted to know what I thought they should be.

As soon as he asked, my mind started reeling off a number of questions that needed to be answered. How much money should you spend on a meal? What kind of car do you rent? How fancy a hotel should you stay in? My list went on and on.

And Charlie had questions of his own. Is it okay for someone to stay over the weekend, when business takes them out of town? (And if it is, who pays for the hotel and meals?) Should you be allowed to charge drinks to your expense voucher? Charlie's list was as long as mine.

I knew we had an official corporate policy, but it was too general to be of much help. It said things like always fly coach if you can, and turn in receipts for anything over $25, but it didn't answer most of the questions we had.

All of a sudden, I knew the answer to all our questions—

and it wasn't going to be found in any corporate handbook. It was the *unwritten* policy that had been in effect for as long as I could remember. *While on the road, maintain the same lifestyle you have at home.* If you normally eat pizza and hamburger, enjoy them when traveling. If you typically dine in finer restaurants, then by all means seek them out when you're on the road.

The policy is consistent down the line. If you drive a luxury car, rent a luxury car. If you normally stay at the best hotels while on vacation, please do so while on business. If you have a drink at night, by all means put it on your T&E.

There are some *special* exceptions. Convenience and efficiency should always be considered. If you will be driving with business associates, you should rent a four-door, mid-size to luxury car (even if you drive a subcompact at home). It will be more convenient for your passengers.

But the basic rule remains the same: Make your choices based on the lifestyle you maintain when you're not at work.

Common sense makes the best sense.

The Moral of the Story

• *Self-control is the best control.* You don't need to waste management time drawing up—and policing—an expense policy if you base yours on common sense. Once people know we expect them to maintain their normal lifestyle when they are traveling for business, we find we have very few problems with T&E.

• *Who can't figure out a way around a policy?* There's another reason you don't want to establish precise guidelines. People will figure out ways to get around them if they don't like them, or don't think they make sense. If you say that the maximum someone can spend for lunch is $10, and he spends $15, he'll hide the extra $5 on his expense account by calling it cab fare. It's just easier—and more effective—to trust your people to do the right thing. If you do, they'll work with you instead of spending their time trying to get around you.

• *Besides, could you find your T&E manual right now?* When people are forced to make a T&E decision, they don't always have their policy manual at hand. (You want to know if the company will pick up the cost of the in-room movie at your hotel, but the T&E manual is back on your desk at work.) If the policy is "do what you would do at home," you can always make the decision quickly and accurately. (Do you have HBO at home?)

• Do *set some guidelines* . . . to make sure the company's image is maintained. Even if people go out for fast food every night when they're at home, we don't want them entertaining clients at a fast-food restaurant. Similarly, we don't want them driving up to a client's office in something they borrowed from Rent-A-Wreck.

25

Organizational Charts and Job Descriptions

When we hire someone, usually one of the first things she'll ask for is our organizational chart. We don't have one. We don't have written job descriptions either.

We haven't had either one for the last twenty-five years, and therein lies a story.

Back in the 1960s, my dad did away with organizational charts and job descriptions, and it was the right thing to do. He believed that written job descriptions encourage people to do only what is written down. Organizational charts, he found, can create barriers between departments and only lead to turf wars.

We've always believed that there is nothing wrong with someone trying to help someone else or another department. That's why there are no organizational charts or job descriptions.

People don't need organizational charts and job descriptions in order to know what to do.

The Moral of the Story

• *Why organizational charts are dumb.* You have to earn the respect of the people you lead. They're not going to follow you just because a piece of paper tells them they're supposed to.

• *Knock down the walls.* If you want people making decisions, and making them quickly, you need to eliminate all visual barriers. That means no closed office doors, no walls between departments, no restrictive lines on the shop floor, and, of course, no organizational charts or job descriptions. Only after you eliminate all of them can you work on the nonvisual impediments to motivation, trust, and quick decision-making.

• *How will people know what to do* . . . if there aren't any job descriptions? That's simple. If you've made your company's goals and objectives clear, people will know what their job is.

26

Who's the Boss?

Talking about why there are no organizational charts may sound good in theory, but how does it work in practice?

Just fine, as Brian Marsh and Dan Bronstetter can tell you.

Brian, sales rep at Preston Phipps, Inc., in Mississagua, Ontario, kept getting complaints from a customer in Canada. The company said the large (four hundred pounds on average) steam traps we sold it weren't working right. The seat, the piece of metal on which the valve sits, kept leaking.

Brian told this to Dan Bronstetter, the assembly department's assistant foreman, who—on his own—called Brian in from the field so they could discuss the problem. Dan didn't have the authority to do that. After all, the reps don't work for the assembly department. But Dan knew there was a problem, and he wanted to get it resolved immediately.

Dan and Brian spent three hours in the shop assembling the trap, and it became clear what was causing the problem. We were shipping the traps to one central location in Canada, and from there the customer would separate the order and send traps to the plants that needed them. However, its shipping department wasn't securing the trap tight enough to the skid, so the trap would move around in transport and the seat became damaged.

Brian told the customer what he and Dan had found. The company immediately changed its shipping procedures, and the problem was solved. The customer was so pleased, in fact, that it wrote Dan a thank-you letter.

If you know how to solve a problem, solve it. Now! Who's in charge, and who has authority over the problem, are secondary. What comes first is resolving the problem.

The Moral of the Story

• *Take action* . . . even if you don't have the authority to do so. Dan did. He called Brian in from the field, and they solved the problem.

• *Cooperate.* Brian could have refused to come. He could have said to Dan, "I don't work for you. Figure out the problem yourself." But he, like Dan, wanted to take care of his customer.

• *If you absolutely must have an organizational chart* . . . telling stories about people taking action, solving problems without authority, becomes even more important. People need to know that dotted lines, showing who reports to whom, aren't the most important thing at the company. Problem solving and taking care of the customer are what really count.

• *We must add value to our products.* You can add value in many ways—through quality, service, speed of delivery, kindness, etc. Dan built the units, so quality was a given. But he did more than that. He *added* value, through service and responsiveness, by calling in Brian. We have to add value wherever possible to satisfy our customers and differentiate ourselves from our competition.

27

Responsible Cheating

Nancy Taggart, who works in the customer service department at our Computrol division, recently received a phone call from one of our dealers. The dealer said he had a customer who needed a part right away, and he couldn't reach his distributor. He asked if Nancy could send the part overnight and then bill the distributor. (The charge then would be included on the invoice the distributor sent the dealer at the end of the month.)

Nancy knew we had discontinued this billing practice, because the distributors had complained. They wanted to control all shipments, to reduce the chances of selling to a bad credit risk.

But even though Nancy knew the rules, she decided to break them, based on the urgency of the situation. The dealer said the customer needed the part immediately, so she sent it out.

It turned out that the dealer wasn't one of his customers, so the local distributor refused to pay. While we would try to get the local dealer to pay us, for the time being we were out the $150 the part cost. To make sure the books balanced, Nancy wrote out a personal check for $150 to cover the cost of the part.

For accepting the responsibility of her cheating (i.e., violating company procedures) and for knowing when to break the rules, we not only gave Nancy her money back, we also gave her a preferred parking spot.

You got to the top by breaking the rules, and "rule-breakers" are exactly the kind of people you should be hiring and promoting.

The Moral of the Story

• *Cheating, that is, breaking the rules, must be encouraged.* I am not talking about violations of moral or legal rules, just bureaucratic ones. And the reason they must be broken is obvious. Policies and procedures will never cover all situations.

• *But you must hold people responsible for their actions.* If you merely say, "We encourage 'cheating,'" you'll be allowing people to do whatever they want regardless of policy.

• *The secret is to reward cheating that furthers your company's goals.* By not only refunding the money, but giving Nancy a preferred parking place, we were saying, "It's okay to break the rules, if the result is satisfying a customer immediately." Satisfying the customer is more important than a bureaucratic procedure covering billing.

28

Why Garfield Had to Die

People spend a lot of time at work, especially here. As you've seen, going above and beyond the call of duty to take care of a customer is pretty commonplace at Armstrong.

If you're going to spend all this time at work, we want you to be comfortable. Your office is your space to do with as you wish. If you want it to be elegant, then we will help you decorate it that way. You want it to be casual, with lots of drawings done by your kids on the walls? That's fine with us, too. We have no rules.

We do, however, ask you to remember where you are, and sometimes your desires and the company's can conflict. It did in the case of one of our receptionists, Doris Blankenship.

Doris did an absolutely wonderful job, but there was one problem. She loved Garfield the cat. The bulletin board behind her desk was covered with Garfield cartoons. She had stuffed Garfields, a Garfield coffee mug—you get the idea.

Now, the first person you see when you go to a company is the receptionist, and here you are visiting Armstrong, which prides itself on high quality and service, and there are Garfields all over the place.

But remember, our culture says your area is yours—and yours alone—so how can I tell Doris that this is not the image we want to project?

I took Doris out to lunch.

"When you and I were working on the phone reports, trying to get people to answer the phone more quickly, you told me that we were not being very professional," I began. "You said people weren't answering the phones quickly enough, and sometimes they were not answering them at all."

"Yes, but we're getting better," she said. "But we have to do more."

"That's great, Doris. You say we are making this place more professional?"

"Yes, we are."

"Well, thank you," I said. "You're a big reason things are improving. What do you think of the Garfields behind you? Do you think they really provide a good image for our company? Do you really think they make us look professional?"

"You're probably right," she said. "They really don't fit here, do they?"

Later that day as I sat in a meeting, I looked out of the conference room window and saw Doris carrying a paper bag with heads and tails hanging out all over the place. She was taking Garfield home.

No one wants to interfere with your rights at work, but others have rights, too. When there are conflicts, common courtesy should prevail.

The Moral of the Story

• *If you have to have pin-ups hanging in the shop . . .* you should take them down before visitors come walking through. Need to have a radio playing at all times? Please wear earphones or turn the volume down. Practicing the Golden Rule can take care of a lot of problems and eliminate the need for a policy manual.

• *What would people say about you if all they saw was your office or work space?* Does it send the right message? If you are in R&D, having prototypes lying around your office makes sense. However, if you walked into an accountant's office and saw papers all over the place, you probably would have a few questions about his ability.

• *Most of the issues about neatness, privacy, and noise* at work can probably be resolved if you just talk to the person involved and ask, "Do you really think your office [behavior] is appropriate for this kind of company?"

Eight

STORIES ABOUT DEALING WITH TROUBLEMAKERS

29

Bozo Cancer

Sometimes you hear a phrase or an analogy that turns on a light in your head. That happened to me recently when I heard someone use the expression "bozo cancer." Let me tell you how the phrase originated and what it means.

I was at Tom Peters' "Skunk Camp," listening to a woman from one of the car companies talking about why being fair to people makes good *business* sense, in addition to being the right thing to do.

"We had to close a plant, but we gave the employees sixty days notice," she said. "What we saw was that productivity actually increased in the last month. If you are fair with people, they'll be fair with you."

Stew Leonard, Jr., from Stew Leonard's grocery store in Connecticut, was in the audience, and he asked, "How do you treat your people fairly, and maintain the culture of the company, while growing at a rapid rate?"

"You can't," she replied. "We've found you cannot bring in fifty people at once, teach them your culture, and expect all fifty to work out. It just doesn't happen, no matter what we do. Out of those fifty, there are going to be five bad apples, and if you keep them they will affect the other forty-five."

Immediately, Chuck Catanig from Apple Computer stood up and said, "We call it 'bozo cancer.'"

"What do you mean?" several people asked at once.

"At Apple, we believe the phrase 'bozo cancer' describes the bad apples. We call it bozo cancer because, like cancer, it spreads. We have found that it's best to cut these bozos out of our company because their negative attitudes affect everyone else."

The jerk stands out. Here's an easy way to identify a bozo. He (or she) is almost *always* involved when you get a complaint—about anything.

The Moral of the Story

• *How do you spot a bozo cancer?* It's simple. The person does not believe in the company's core values, vision statement, style of leadership, and culture, and generally has a bad attitude.

• *How patient can you afford to be?* Some negative people can be turned around, but you can't afford to wait too long. The more power a bozo has to damage your company —either through the amount of money she's responsible for or the number of people she's in charge of—the quicker you have to move.

• *There is only one way to deal with bozo cancer.* Cut it out before it spreads.

• *Bozo cancer can also work in reverse.* Just as your people can be affected by a bozo, they can also be affected by leaders who are happy, creative, and hardworking. Positive leaders are also contagious.

30

The S.O.B.

Sometimes the boss can be a bozo, too. Let me tell you a story about it.

An upper-level manager came into the department with high credentials. He had all the answers to our problems. He even had answers to problems that nobody knew we had. Within weeks he made it clear that he, the new department head, was smarter and better than us all. He knew everything.

I can remember working in this department and reporting to this S.O.B. He would give me a project and explain in general terms what he wanted done. Each time I started to work, I realized I didn't know exactly what should be done, and so I'd go back for more instructions. He'd explain again—this time with some disappointment in his voice—but there never seemed to be enough details for me to do the job right, and so I'd have to go back to him a third, and sometimes a fourth or fifth, time. Each time I came back, he became angrier and made me feel more and more inadequate. I started to doubt my ability to do anything right.

I talked to other people in the department about my problem, and they all said the same thing. "He does this to everyone. Don't let it bother you. He always explains things as ambiguously as possible."

"Why would he do that?" I asked.

"So he can make you feel inferior to him. He wants you to fear him."

This went on for years, until people in the S.O.B.'s department couldn't take it anymore. They approached upper management and asked that the S.O.B. be fired. Management took the request seriously, since this department had always been happy and productive prior to the S.O.B.'s arrival. He was asked to leave.

Managers should delegate as much as they can, with few exceptions. One pivotal exception: hiring. Look at it this way: If you hire someone for a $35,000-a-year position, she is going to cost you a minimum of $700,000 over the next twenty years. *You* are the one who should be making $700,000 decisions.

The Moral of the Story

• *Play matchmaker.* Match the personality of the person you're hiring with those of the people he'll be working with. If they are not compatible, there's bound to be trouble. No matter how brilliant he is, or how impressive his grades, titles, or past experience, *never* hire an individual unless he will get along with the people he'll be working with.

• *Happy people work harder.* People enjoy working with people they like. And they'll work harder for them.

• *Be tough* and *fair.* People will still respect you, even after you make a decision that's not popular—providing that you're fair. Don't be the nice boss that never makes a tough or unpopular decision; you won't be respected.

31

Did You Hear the Latest Rumor?

Dan, Tom, and Jerry were having lunch one day when the conversation changed from football to things they had heard were going to happen in the company.

"Did you hear Armstrong is going to buy XYZ company?" asked Tom.

"No, I heard the Armstrong family is going to sell the business," said Dan.

"That's funny, I heard through the grapevine that Armstrong is going to move the factory to Florida." Jerry chuckled.

Dan said, "Where do these rumors come from? Who thinks them up? I wonder how they get this information?"

Jerry laughed again. "These are the same stories I heard eight or ten years ago. You remember, that's when the Armstrong family moved to Florida."

"That's right. I remember that," said Tom.

"I don't know why I listen to these rumors. They're never right," Dan said angrily.

We will never be able to stop rumors; they're here to stay, like telling jokes and good stories.

But where jokes create laughter, and stories show the way things should be done, rumors only cause confusion, uncertainty, and stress. That is never healthy. If we better understand why rumors start, maybe we can help prevent them.

I believe most rumors are a direct result of someone telling somebody information he doesn't need to know. Don't tell somebody something unless there is a *need* for him to know it. Otherwise, you're starting a rumor.

How can you tell if she needs to know? That's simple. Just ask yourself: "Does this piece of information affect the other person's job, or a project she may be working on?" If it does, tell her. If not, don't.

Loose lips sink morale. If there is no legitimate business reason to pass along a piece of information, don't.

The Moral of the Story

• *Tell a story, instead of a rumor.* Rumors have cost Armstrong an acquisition, plus management's time and needless stress on countless occasions. Rumors hurt, and you are a source of the pain if you start or spread them. Tell a story instead. It's better for everyone.

• *Remember the kid's game "Telephone"?* Every time a rumor is repeated, it changes. Can you imagine what it sounds like after being repeated for the tenth time?

• *If you have to spread a rumor, spread a good rumor.* Good news motivates people toward success. There's enough competition out there; we don't need more—in the form of rumors—coming from within our company.

• *How do you deal with a rumor?* If someone sees something or hears something that causes him to jump to conclusions, deal with it. Immediately. Answer all his questions. If a rumor has become widespread, call a meeting to discuss it. Don't try to stop the rumor with a memo. People need to see your face, hear your voice, and watch your body language.

Nine

STORIES TO HONOR QUALITY AND SERVICE

32

Japanese Grocery Shopping

I had been told that in Japan quality is perceived by the appearance of the product. I discovered this was true when I decided to go grocery shopping in Tokyo.

The first aisle contained fruits and vegetables, and I immediately saw the pride in the produce come through in the packaging. The first item I looked at was a cantaloupe (perfect in color) with its stem extending three inches and tied with a decorative twist at the end. The cantaloupe was packed in a special container that allowed easy inspection. Next I looked at the strawberries. They weren't thrown into a pint container as they are here, rather, they were each positioned individually within the box. All were bright red without a single imperfection. The onions had no skin fraying at the edges, and there was no dirt on them. The stems were individually cut for uniformity. The cauliflowers were small, but there were no brown spots to be found, and they looked as if they had been freshly picked and washed.

Over in the meat department, the famous Kobe beef was on display. Each piece of Kobe was perfectly sliced and presented on a tray made of *china*. The chicken was not piled up on a plate or placed several pieces to a package.

Instead, each piece of chicken was in its own package. The window to the freezer case was clean. There were no fingerprint smudges or dust.

When I went to the checkout counter with my items, I was surprised to see there were no lines. There were two girls behind each counter—one to ring up the order, the other to bag. They didn't use ordinary paper bags. Rather, the items were placed in a decorative paper bag similar to the kind you receive at an expensive store during the Christmas holidays.

My shopping trip wasn't exactly like going to the local grocery store.

No one ever said you had to compete on price.

The Moral of the Story

• *Quality is in the eye of the beholder.* The Japanese perceive quality through a product's package, so the packaging and presentation are as good as they possibly can be. Imagine what their standards must be on items such as cars, computers, televisions, and, of course, steam traps.

• *It is* their *perception that matters.* A company that is truly international adopts its markets' definition of quality, instead of trying to impose its own standards.

• *But doesn't this cost money?* Sure. But you only have to compete on price, if that's the niche you're in. Most people appreciate, and are willing to pay for, quality.

• *Just a thought.* Remember thirty years ago when you went to the store with your mother and she wouldn't let you buy toys stamped "made in Japan," because "made in Japan" was another way of saying "junk"?

33

You Get What You Pay For—or Do You?

Our company car may have been designed by listening to thousands of consumers, have "advanced engineering," and have been voted "car of the year," but you can't prove it by me.

After a long trip, I returned late one night to the Palm Beach International Airport and walked out to my car. I opened the convenient tail hatch and threw my luggage in the back. I remember thinking how nice it was to have all this space for luggage.

As I pulled out of my parking space, I realized I had a flat tire. No problem, I thought. In ten minutes, I'd be back on my way. But then it hit me. I had never seen a spare in the car. Rummaging around in the dark, I found where it was hidden. Even better, I saw the jack.

The bracket holding the tire and jack to the car came complete with a T handle to loosen the nut, which I thought was a great idea. As I grabbed the handle, I noticed it was cracked. My guess is a factory worker had overtightened the nut, cracking the handle, when he attached the spare.

"Okay, David, just turn the handle slowly and easily and it won't break."

It broke.

There I am at 8 P.M. on a Saturday, forty miles from home, with a flat tire. I have a spare tire and jack, but no way to get the tire free for installation.

As I sat there fuming, I thought: They talk about "quality," but if they believe it, why didn't they make a better handle, and why didn't the QA department catch the defect? More important, why didn't the factory worker replace the T handle? He had to know he cracked it by over-tightening.

Because the quality on a little thing was not done right, I sat waiting for what seemed like forever for a tow truck to change my flat.

The Air Force has a good idea. It periodically requires the people who pack parachutes to make jumps. There is no quality problem with the way the chutes are packed.

The Moral of the Story

• *If you preach quality . . .* you'll have to practice it everywhere. People will judge your product on every part, even the handle that holds the spare in place.

• *Quality must be number 1 for everyone.* Not just for the people in QA, but for every single person who handles the product or deals with a customer. In this case, the purchasing department should have bought a better handle; people who saw the crack as the car passed down the line should have flagged the problem, and even the salesman who presented me the car should have checked to see that everything—including the spare—was okay.

• *If quality is your number one job,* look to improve your quality in a thousand small ways instead of through one huge technological leap. Your chances of satisfying your customer will be 999 times greater if you do.

• *Quality is more noticeable in the small things.* It's very important that things we use every day—like a radio knob on a car, or the turn signal—work right. Otherwise people will be constantly reminded that your product is not as good as it should be.

34

Quality Is in the Eye of the Beholder

The Japanese are well known for demanding quality in imported goods. Their standards are so high that many American companies, even those known in the United States for their quality, have been unable to break into the Japanese market.

Armstrong is known for selling nothing but the best, but even we had problems in Japan—at first. But instead of giving up, we viewed their demands as a challenge. Let me tell you about the challenges we met.

When we first started selling steam traps in Japan, we received complaints about how our traps looked. Japanese customers expect no scratches, blemishes, or color distortions on their products. So we now use a paint that has more pigment and produces a richer-looking paint job. We now also package the traps *individually* so they will not bump up against one another in shipping.

The Japanese also complained about the inside of our traps. They said there were burrs in the threads (of maybe one out of a hundred traps) and that the metal finish on the inside of the traps looked too coarse. Again, neither of those things would affect the traps' performance, but we changed to meet their demands. We told the foundry to use wet sand and wash the core with chemicals to give the inside of the trap a smoother look, and we had all the burrs on the thread removed by hand.

We even went beyond their demands and changed the printing on the tags that identify the traps. Before, they had been done by hand. Now the lettering is done by machine, which improves its quality.

Not all of our changes, though, were cosmetic. The Japanese require each trap to be steam tested before it is shipped. We air test all of our traps, and traditionally only steam test a random sample, because steam testing is expensive. Now we steam test every one to comply with the customers' demand.

During my last trip to Japan, our customers praised us for our improvements in quality.

I don't define quality. You don't define quality. The customer defines quality, and the customer's definition is the only thing that matters.

The Moral of the Story

• *It's different over there.* A true international company listens to its overseas customers instead of dictating to them.

• *You have to meet their standards.* We make a great product. Our quality is considered number one in our industry, but that simply isn't good enough if a customer—either here or overseas—wants us to do more. To keep its business, and its trust, we have to meet whatever standards it sets for us.

• *But how can you afford to do all this?* The answer, in most cases, involves trade-offs, and in some case you simply have to charge more. Using a better grade of paint costs more, but if that's important to the customer and product support isn't, since it has its own technical staff, maybe we can paint the traps twice and eliminate the support. In cases where a customer wants everything—and more—what we usually say is, "We're happy to do everything you ask, but it is going to cost a little bit more for all this service and all those enhancements. Is that okay?" The customer will either agree to the price increase or agree to places where we can cut back.

35

Sweetened Ice Tea

It was a hot day in July. A salesman, Jon Bingaman, and I had just finished making a sales call, and while driving to our next appointment we decided to stop and get a cold drink. We pulled into a truck stop restaurant. I ordered an ice tea.

"Could you bring me some Sweet 'N Low with that, please?" I asked.

"The sugar is on the table," the waitress replied.

"Yes, but it doesn't dissolve in ice tea as well as Sweet 'N Low does," I told her.

"I'm sorry, that's all we have."

When the waitress came back with our drinks, she placed a small metal cup down next to my ice tea.

"I'm sorry we don't have any Sweet 'N Low," she said. "But I took hot water and poured it over some sugar to help dissolve it. I hope that's okay."

Now that's service!

On the way out, I went up to the waitress and gave her a $2 tip for my 60-cent ice tea, and I thanked her for the best service I'd had in a long time.

You should have seen her coworkers' expressions. I must have told this story over fifty times.

There is no such thing as a commodity. Everything—even a glass of ice tea—can be differentiated on service.

The Moral of the Story

• *Good service will generate future business.* Will I eat at that truck stop the next time I'm in the area? You bet. Will I tell everyone I know about the service I received? I already have. I've told this story fifty times.

• *Good service should exist everywhere.* Remember I got this service at a truck stop, not a five-star restaurant. At Armstrong good service should be found in every department, not just sales.

• *Good service should be rewarded.* If we see a colleague providing good service, we should praise her. If we receive good service, we should do everything possible to encourage it. I made a point of making a big deal out of the service I received, in front of the waitress' coworkers. I also gave her a 333 percent tip.

36

Trash-Can
Service

Monty Wood, production and inventory control manager, took his family to Epcot Center at Disney World. After enjoying many of the rides and exhibits, they decided to have lunch.

After lunch, while they were walking to the next attraction, Monty's daughter suddenly realized she had left her dental retainer on the picnic table. But when they got back to the table, the retainer was gone.

Thinking that maybe the retainer had been thrown away, Monty walked over to the trash can. But it had already been emptied. Unwilling to give up, Monty found a custodian and told him he thought the retainer was probably in the trash that had been hauled away. The custodian showed Monty where the garbage was kept. There were bags upon bags upon bags and no way of telling which trash container they had come from. It looked hopeless.

"I'll tell you what," the custodian said. "I'll get approval from my supervisor and see if we can get some people out here to go through the garbage."

"You're kidding," said Monty.

"No, I'm not. Let me get my supervisor."

The supervisor came over and told Monty he'd get a crew to go through the trash that night.

"You can really do that?" Monty asked.

"We do it all the time for our customers," the supervisor said.

"I can't believe you're really going to do this," Monty said as he wrote down his address and phone number for the supervisor.

Two weeks later, Monty received a letter from the supervisor. Not only did the crew try, but they had the courtesy of notifying Monty about what they did. Unfortunately, they didn't find the retainer. The effort, however, was deeply appreciated.

No matter how small or insignificant a service the customer requests, always remember the customer perceives it to be important. Otherwise, she wouldn't have asked for it.

The Moral of the Story

CAN YOU FIGURE OUT WHAT THE MORALS ARE?

- _____
  _____
  _____
  _____

- _____
  _____
  _____
  _____

How do your morals compare with mine?

• Everyone *must take care of the customer*. Customer service is extremely important and must be practiced at all levels by *everyone*. Here we see the custodians providing excellent customer service.

• *Practice what you preach*. The supervisor assigned a crew to search through the garbage. Talk is cheap; action says it all. The supervisor's decision also showed his employees that he was serious about providing good service.

• *The word will spread*. Monty has probably told this story to five or ten people. Just think of the good publicity and goodwill Epcot and its people are receiving.

37

"You Want It When?"

This story has a happy ending, but you wouldn't have thought so, given the way it began. It began with a problem. A big one.

Our Armstrong-Yoshitake plant had been unable to ship some orders because a key part was not in inventory. Armstrong-Yoshitake prides itself on having the fastest turn-around time in the industry (standard delivery time for these orders is three days) and the orders were now several weeks old.

Tom Rockwell, the sales specialist who had sold the order, decided to see what he could do to help get the shipment out the door. He went to see foreman Gary Vedmore.

"Gary, what's the problem?" Tom asked. "The order should have shipped weeks ago."

"We're swamped," said Gary. "There's just no way we can get to it for another couple of weeks."

Tom knew that was unacceptable, and he asked if he could machine the parts himself and finish his office work later. Gary had Bill D. Hartman, a machinist, show Tom what to do so he wouldn't get hurt. In addition to doing his own job that day, Bill kept checking to see that Tom was okay.

He was. He made all the necessary parts that day, and the orders went out the next morning.

Everyone, including the boss, must be prepared to drop everything to satisfy a customer.

The Moral of the Story

• *Keep your word.* If you say an order will ship on time, do everything in your power to make sure that it does.

• *Make sure that everyone knows what his job is*—satisfying the customer. Manufacturing the part was more important than anything else Tom might have done in the office that day.

• *Teamwork, teamwork, teamwork.* Tom helped Gary. Bill Hartman helped Tom. Everybody *says* we must become more competitive. We must respond faster to our customers and we must be known as *the* service provider in our industry, but unless everybody *does* something about it, it will never happen.

• *You are the company.* Customers usually don't view companies as a bunch of buildings and a mailing address somewhere. They see companies as the people they deal with. To Tom's customers, Tom is Armstrong-Yoshitake. He had to take the responsibility of getting the order out.

38

Dr. Deming
Would Be Proud

KerCHUNK. KerCHUNK. KerCHUNK.

That noise told Bill C. Hartman, punch press foreman, that the Minster 250-ton press had been turned on. As Bill watched, rolls of stainless steel were fed into the machine and finished parts exited the other end. By the sound of the machine and the frequency of the kerCHUNKs, Bill could tell the press was running fine.

A few hours went by, and Bill walked over to press operator Bob Kirchner.

"Isn't it time that someone from the tool room came over and polished the rings on the die?"

"No," Bob said. "It doesn't need polishing. Everything is running great."

"How many pieces have you run so far?" Bill asked.

"Over 2,000."

"Well, keep a close eye on the tolerances and when they get bad, give the tool room a call."

At the end of the day, Bill asked Bob how many pieces he had run.

"Over 7,200."

Bill was amazed.

"Don't we normally run about 300 pieces an hour?"

"Right."

"But Bob, if you did 7,200 pieces, you averaged 900 parts per hour during the eight-hour shift; that's triple what we normally do. How's that possible?"

"The quality of the coil stock is so good that we don't need tool and die makers to keep coming by to polish the draw rings all day long. If you don't have to constantly shut the machine down for polishing, you can run a lot more parts."

By the end of the week, we had run over 36,000 parts through the Minster 250-ton press, instead of the usual 12,000. All the parts were within tolerance.

Bill called down to purchasing and asked them to find out from the vendor if they had any more of this kind of steel in their warehouse.

"They say they have two coils remaining," came the response.

"Do whatever it takes, but get those coils into the plant now. This stuff is great."

A penny *saved* reducing quality is not a penny earned.

The Moral of the Story

• *Dr. Deming was right.* His primary message was that if you improve quality, you improve productivity, and we proved it here. By improving the quality of the steel we used, we could run the machine for a longer period without having to shut it down to polish the dies.

• *And look what happens if you improve quality.* If you improve productivity through higher quality, you can reduce your price. That allows you to increase market share. And by increasing market share, you can add more jobs. The few extra pennies per pound that the new steel cost were more than offset by the increase in productivity.

• *Quality is a continuous journey.* We were already paying a premium for quality coil stock, but obviously a better material existed. We had just missed it. By switching to the better coil, we had one more opportunity to improve our quality.

Ten

STORIES TO HONOR PARTNERSHIPS

39

The Endangered Buffalo

We've all heard or read about the days when the buffalo roamed through the Western prairies. But over time, the buffalo became endangered and almost extinct.

American industry has its buffalo—steel mills. Once they dominated the American business community, much like the buffalo ruled the prairie, but in the 1970s Japan and other foreign countries entered the U.S. market with comparable quality and far lower prices. Unable to compete, most U.S. steel mills became extinct. But Carpenter Steel survived because it worked as a partner with its customers, delivering quality goods and service on time.

Armstrong was doing business with Carpenter Steel long before the foreign mills came into the United States, and we stayed with the company, even though its prices were higher.

Time passed and the tables were turned. Foreign mills were no longer able to keep up with demand from American industry, and once again Carpenter Steel had American companies knocking on its door.

Soon a customer offered Carpenter Steel an order "too

good to be true." It would buy several million dollars' worth of steel at a *premium* price if Carpenter could deliver immediately. To fulfill the order, Carpenter would have had to delay shipments to its current customers—one of which was Armstrong. Carpenter turned the offer down.

This is a lifetime partnership, one that will work both ways.

You really do get what you pay for.

The Moral of the Story

• *Partnership is not just about price, quality, or service.* It's also about commitment, loyalty, and all those other "soft" things. Armstrong stuck by Carpenter Steel during tough times, a sign of loyalty and commitment. We were even willing to pay a higher price for its products. Carpenter Steel reciprocated when times were good. It turned down a large order with great profit margins, and did not raise its price to Armstrong. This was how it showed its loyalty and commitment to us.

• *You are whom you do business with.* The better companies always seem to have better companies as their suppliers. It's no accident. Doing business with the best allows them to maintain their standards. Wherever possible, Armstrong only uses the best suppliers.

• *Long-term commitments outweigh the big order.* Every time. That big order is gone once you fill it. Partnerships can last forever.

• *If you are spending an awful lot of time with your vendor talking about price and terms . . .* then you don't have a *partnership*.

40

It's Free
for the Taking

Our purchasing manager, Jerry Phelps, like the rest of our executives, is constantly being asked to look for ways to cut costs. Yet at the same time, we tell everyone, "Save that money, without jeopardizing the relationships we have with our vendors." We want our vendors to be partners, and we never want to go with the lowest bidder just because it is the lowest bidder.

Jerry found an unique idea to reconcile both these goals.

In our lobby he's placed a table covered with drawings of things we dream of manufacturing—but haven't yet, because of some problem. Maybe we haven't figured out a way to get the product up to our standards, or we're baffled about how to add a feature. Sometimes we haven't produced the product because it will just cost too much. The hope is when vendors visit our company they'll take a copy of the drawings with them and call us back with a quote when they've solved the problem.

We've never heard of another company where the purchasing department provides information to its vendors in such a unique way. Normally, vendors must request a list of items they can bid on before they're given drawings. With this new approach, vendors only have to take the time to pick up the drawings.

If you don't have the answer, find someone who does, recognizing that the someone might be outside your company. Your suppliers have a vested interest in your success. Take advantage of their expertise.

The Moral of the Story

• *"We want our vendors to be our partners"* is more than the business saying of the moment. It should be your operating philosophy. Constantly draw on their resources in solving problems.

• *Innovations come in many forms.* They can be new products, but as Jerry Phelps has shown, they can also be new ideas. *Every* department can come up with innovations.

• *Partnerships work both ways.* If you want to have the resources of your vendors to draw on, they have to know you are not going to squeeze them for every nickel. If you do, they'll spend their time helping solve someone else's problems.

• *It's not always about money.* While we are always interested in cutting costs, that is not the only thing we call on our vendors for. Sometimes we ask them to help find ways to improve quality, add a feature, or get the product to the customer faster.

41

Train Your Vendors

During a recent staff meeting at the Three Rivers plant, several topics were discussed, including how the company came across when we appeared on a cable TV show and what we were going to do about improving the appearance of our lobby.

Jeanette Whitney, secretary to the general manager, put the two thoughts together. Why don't we, she asked, have a tape of the TV show running continuously in the lobby?

What a great idea! Here was a way to show our vendors what Armstrong was all about. (And the fact that an executive secretary came up with—and was willing to express—the idea just underscored the point.)

As you have seen, we do business differently from other companies. Showing the video in the lobby is yet another way of convincing vendors that while we certainly want a low-price supplier, we would rather have a partner—one that understands the way we do business.

Your vendors can be an important asset. Use them.

The Moral of the Story

• *Don't forget about your vendors.* We talk all the time about the need to train our employees, sales force, and managers, but what about our vendors? We must show them what we want: a partnership where they contribute goods and services of only the highest quality. They are never going to know that unless we tell them, and show them with things like the video in the lobby.

• *The open door policy should be company-wide.* We have no rules saying that vendors can talk only to people in our purchasing department. They are encouraged by our purchasing department to talk to whomever they want at Armstrong, in order to understand better both how we do business and what we need.

• *Don't stop here.* Constantly communicate with your vendors. We do. We send them thank-you notes to reinforce what they've done right, and even copies of our stories so they can learn a little bit more about us. When they come in, we also try to show them around. We want them to know that they *must* meet our standards, or we will find someone else who will, even if that someone else is going to cost us a few dollars more.

Eleven

STORIES TO TURN US INTO CHANGE-GOURMETS

42

"Shut Up and Eat Your M&Ms"

My problem was simple: How was I going to get people to accept new ideas?

Change is always threatening. When things change, people don't know where they stand. It's not surprising, then, that people invariably resist change.

We all know that. Yet we need to keep adapting to an ever-changing marketplace.

What do you do?

My solution then was to hand out M&Ms. My solution now is to tell the M&M story.

It all started when I learned about a heat-sensitive paint that changes color with temperature. I got to wondering if there was a way we could use it on any of our products.

I knew what the initial reaction of our senior engineers and salespeople would be: "It's too gimmicky. We sell engineered products."

"Our current paint is good enough."

"Why would we ever want to fool around with something like that?"

To make sure I didn't hear those kinds of things, I told

everyone at the meeting that we were here to discuss *new* ideas, and then I handed everyone a M&M. "You are allowed one negative comment during the meeting," I said. "Once you make that comment, you must eat your M&M. If you don't have a M&M in front of you, you can't say anything negative."

It was great! Instead of being threatened by new ideas, people supported them. Anything negative was instantly met with a joking "Shut up and eat your M&M."

We even got a new product idea out of it—steam traps that change color when they stop working. We're now testing ten of them in the plant belonging to one of our major customers.

I'm buying more M&Ms.

Minds are like parachutes: They only function when open.

The Moral of the Story

• *Disarming can be charming.* Direct orders from the boss saying "change your behavior" rarely work for long. If I simply said, "From this day forward, you can only make constructive comments at meetings," I doubt that things would have improved. But introducing the M&Ms changed all that. Instead of being threatened by new ideas, everybody now supports them—or at least seriously listens to them.

• *Sometimes shock treatment is called for . . .* and giving everyone a M&M did shock them. You have to get people's attention. I needed a way to let people know that I was serious about having them support new ideas. Change can be uncomfortable at first, but you can get used to any-thing given enough time.

• *If you want people to be creative,* you *have to be cre-ative.* I keep telling people to look for new and innovative ways of solving problems. This story, I hope, gave them an example.

43

Make Me a Copy

We all have them—those beautiful, wonderful, efficient, time-saving machines called copiers. I'll bet we have as many as you do, maybe more. Every time I turn a corner in one of our buildings, I find another copier. A few years ago, we had one basic copier that had few functions and could produce only a limited number of pages at a time, and it served a division of three hundred people perfectly well. Today, copiers are more complex and more flexible, and can print even faster, and we have *seven of them* for the same three hundred people. It's absurd.

We tried limiting access to the copiers and charging the cost per copy back to the department that used the machine, in the hope of eliminating excess copying, but nothing worked. We were addicted to our copying machines.

One day I found myself in a staff meeting presenting a crazy idea.

"What if we removed two of [the seven] copiers?" I said. "Think of all the money we'd save. We'd buy less paper, less toner, and less ink; there would be two fewer maintenance agreements; less capital tied up in the copiers; we'd be mailing fewer copies, so our postage bill would be less; there'd be less time spent filing and reading copies, so our productivity would go up." The list went on and on.

I was sure my suggestion would be hooted down. But to my surprise, everyone took my idea one step further. Instead of removing two machines, *they wanted to shut them all down* during the first and third weeks in the month.

"That scares me, and I'm fearless," I said.

We reached a compromise. The machines were turned off every day between 1 P.M. and 4 P.M.

Want an easy way to save money? Pull the plug on your copiers.

The Moral of the Story

• *Once you become a copy junkie . . .* it's hard to break the habit. I really feel it's an addiction. Copiers, which were once a benefit to our company, are now quite probably a detriment. The best way I know to break the copying habit is by going cold turkey—shutting down the machines.

• *Don't "cc" the boss.* My contribution to eliminating needless copies was to tell everyone not to "carbon" me on anything unless I specifically asked for it. For those people who didn't hear me, or didn't believe me, or simply didn't want to change, I began stamping, in red ink, unwanted copies that ended up on my desk with the message "Not required reading, don't copy David Armstrong." The message got out.

• *Shred your routing lists.* One simple way to eliminate copies is to eliminate all routing and distribution lists for reports. If you require people to ask for specific pieces of information, you'll find the number of copies you need drops dramatically. If you aren't willing to make this a blanket policy, try it out on a limited basis. For the next three months, have all copies of reports sent to one person. She'll be the keeper of the reports and if you need a copy, you'll have to ask her. Any report that is not consistently asked for can be eliminated.

• *What reports have you eliminated today?* If you answered "none," you haven't looked closely enough. We *all* have reports we can do without. Your company, and your job, change over time. If your reports haven't changed, they are probably useless.

44

Batteries, Batteries, Who's Got the Batteries?

One day Warren Tase, a product engineer at Armstrong Machine Works, needed a new battery for his calculator. He walked over to the purchasing department and checked the filing cabinet where the batteries had always been kept. They weren't there.

"Where are you keeping the batteries these days?" he asked Diane Reece, the department secretary.

"We stopped stocking batteries, because employees in the shop were always taking them to use in their radios," she replied. "I'll be happy to order some for you. How many did you need? They'll be here in a day or so."

"I can't wait that long," Warren said, starting to raise his voice. "I need them now! I have a project to finish."

With that, Warren got in his car and drove downtown and bought the nine-volt battery he needed.

When he got back to the office, Warren filled out and submitted an expense report for $3.82 to cover the cost of his trip downtown. (The battery cost $2.98, and at 21 cents a mile, Warren's four-mile round trip added another 84 cents.)

When head controller Ken Clay got the expense voucher, he called Warren and said, "Do you realize how much it's going to cost the company to process this?"

"I am aware of the cost," said Warren, "but I thought you—and the other executives—should be aware of the policy of not stocking batteries."

Become an emotional, *public* hater of petty bureaucracy. Be outrageous if you have to. You can never have a truly efficient company if you're forcing people to put up with Mickey Mouse rules.

The Moral of the Story

• *Sometimes you have to be dramatic.* Warren was not trying to nickel-and-dime the company in asking for $3.82. He was trying to make a point. There are often Mickey Mouse rules that need to be abolished if a company is to become more efficient. But changing the rules, especially when they have been in place a long time, is not easy. Dramatizing the problem, as Warren did in asking to be reimbursed for both the cost of the battery and his mileage, can bring the problem to the fore.

• *Be a nuisance.* In a world that becomes more competitive by the hour, we don't have time for petty bureaucracy. My suggestion? Become a nuisance. Be an emotional, *public* hater of bureaucracy. Rant and rave. Tear up papers. Be outrageous. Let people know that we no longer have time to put up with silly bureaucratic rules.

• *When are you going to retire Mickey Mouse?* How many unproductive rules or procedures do you have in your company? What are you going to do about them? Isn't it time for something to change?

45

What We Learned from Our College "Scholarship" Program

What was once a good idea can become hopelessly outdated when circumstances change. That's something I learned from our college "scholarship" program.

Many companies offer college scholarships and loans to students. We don't. Instead, we'll help all employees' children pay for school by *guaranteeing* them a summer job. My grandfather started this program, and we've been very happy with it. Not only does it help kids pay for school, but it also serves as a training program. During their four summers (plus winter and spring breaks, if they want) students get a chance to see how we do things. There's a benefit to us, too. We use the program as a way of spotting new talent.

The only problem with the program is the way the work is divided. Ever since we began hiring college students, boys have worked in the shop—some of our parts weigh more than a hundred pounds—and the young women work in the office.

Well, when we first set up the program, years and years ago, more boys than girls went to college, so the division of labor made sense. We always had more jobs in the shop than we did in the office.

But times change. The percentage of young women attending college has steadily increased over the years, and some summers we employed more girls than boys. When that happened, we frequently found ourselves making work for the college girls, having them planting flowers, sweeping floors, washing windows, and cleaning out files. This at a time when we were often short-handed in the shop. The old division of labor wasn't helping anyone.

It wasn't hard to figure out what to do. You'll now find college women working in the shop. If they can't lift something, they ask for help.

Things change. Periodically—at least every three years— you must reexamine every rule and procedure to see if it still makes sense.

The Moral of the Story

• *Don't lose the meanings of your programs.* Over time, programs and ways of doing business become ingrained, and you take them for granted. Set up a system of review so you double-check to see that your programs are still accomplishing what you want them to. We wanted *all* our college students to learn about business, but it was clear, when we stopped to think about it, the women weren't. The experience of planting flowers is only beneficial if you plan to open your own flower shop.

• *Always ask, "Why?"* Perhaps the best time to question a program is the first time you hear about it. When someone explains a procedure to you, ask, "Why do we do things that way?" If I had asked that the first time someone told me about our summer college program, we might have changed things sooner.

• *If you like the parents . . .* you'll probably like the kids. I've found as a rule that the children of our best workers also tend to be good workers. That's an important reason we continue our summer college program each year.

• *Teach the children.* What better training and advice can we give our future labor force than offering them a job for the summer? After 40 hours a week, 160 hours a month, 480 during an entire summer, they'll have a pretty good idea about what they like and don't like about a job. That will help them enormously in figuring out what they want to do with their life.

Twelve

STORIES TO
BOOST
CREATIVITY

46

I'm Happy They're All Laughing at Me

You never want people to forget about you or the things that you sell. With that in mind, let me tell you about three things we did recently to ensure people were always thinking about us.

When we introduced the Silver Nugget, a radiator trap part that is about the size of a silver dollar, I had a bunch of them painted different colors. I had little hooks attached to them and sent them out to the sales force a month before Christmas, with a note saying that they made perfect Christmas ornaments. I hoped that their children would see the Silver Nuggets hanging from their tree and ask "What's that, Daddy?" reminding our people to sell Silver Nuggets that day.

I was really excited about a new lift trap we had created, but was worried people would forget that we had it. Since each trap weighs 280 pounds, we had to store it at a warehouse away from the office, and it's true: out of sight, out of mind. Well, I made sure that didn't happen. I had the first lift trap—all 280 pounds of it—placed in the center of sales manager Ray Masnari's office. I had another one delivered to John Bingaman, the person who would help sell and solve application problems. I told them both that the traps would stay where they were until the company had sold fifty of them. It got their attention—and the traps sold in record time.

We were having a problem promoting our new unit heaters. In the summer, nobody needs heat, so there is a tendency not to push the product. In winter, when the salesmen made their calls, being creatures of habit, they often forgot to talk about the heaters.

I mailed two postcards that took care of the problem. In the first—mailed two months before the cold season began—the unit heater, wearing sunglasses and a floppy hat, was shown lying on a beach towel. A beautiful young lady in a bikini was nearby. On the back of the card it said, "I'm enjoying my summer vacation. I'm looking forward to seeing you again. I'll be back in town in the near future. Please don't forget me." It was signed "Mr. Unit Heater."

A few weeks later, our salespeople got a second postcard. This time the unit heater was wearing an overcoat. The message? "I'm coming home. The cold season is here. I'm ready to go to work. Give me a call."

The cards created a lot of attention—and a lot of business.

If people aren't laughing at your ideas, you aren't being creative enough. If no one is challenging (scoffing, giggling at) your ideas, you are playing it too safe.

The Moral of the Story

• *The unusual gets people's attention.* While not all our salesmen would have taken the time to read a memo reminding them to sell unit heaters, everybody had the time to read the postcards.

• *If you need reassurance . . .* think of the invention of the telephone or television or the airplane. The initial reaction to a "flying machine" was a loud round of guffaws.

• *And suppose* you're *wrong.* So what? In order to support "fast failures" and "small starts," we have to talk— and indeed laugh—about our failures. That's the best way to let people know it's okay to try.

47

Our Toilet-Paper Secret

Has this ever happened to you? You've come up with an idea that you're really excited about. I mean *really excited!* But there's a problem. You can't get it approved. You try and you try to get people to support it, but no matter what you do nobody gets behind it. Most of us, after a period of time, just stop trying.

But Rich Hitz is not like most people. Rich, the head of R&D (now president of Geo. B. Allan & Co.), had figured out a way to use a revolutionary kind of steam trap on paper dryers. Rich knew his idea would work, but no matter what he did, he could never interest the president enough to take a look at his research, which proved the product would be a big seller.

Understanding that the president was very busy, Rich needed a creative way to grab his attention. He decided to write his report on a roll of toilet paper and send it to the boss.

An interesting thing happened. The president read the report—and approved Rich's idea.

Consider the postage stamp: It sticks to one thing until it's done.

The Moral of the Story

• *Before you can inspire others . . .* you have to be inspired yourself. Make sure you have answered every potential question and have proof your idea will work. Unless you are enthusiastic, can prove your idea works, and have something unique—like toilet paper—to catch people's attention, it is going to be very difficult to sell your idea, no matter how good it sounds.

• *There are very few ideas that sell themselves.* So the next time you have an idea that you're really enthused about, but you can't get management's attention, don't give up. Find a way to be heard, just as Rich did with his toilet paper.

• *Self-interest is the best interest.* Most people will be positive and motivated when putting forward an idea of their own. When pitching an idea to a superior, present it in a way that appeals to *her* self-interest.

48

The Résumé

A board of directors needed a new member. Several résumés had been received, but one clearly stood out. It didn't have the usual information about where the applicant went to school, what companies he was an officer of, or what awards he had received. Instead, this résumé showed how and what the applicant thought: He had submitted a storybook.

Can you guess who this person was?

Imagination is more important than knowledge.
—ALBERT EINSTEIN

The Moral of the Story

- *I am what I am.* I submitted the storybook because it was the best way I could communicate my philosophies to strangers. It explains, in great detail, how I think a business should be run and how I expect people to act. No "traditional" résumé could have done that in sufficient detail.

• *Creativity can be difficult for people to accept.* Don't let that stop you. If a person or company can't accept your creative ideas, or the way you go about your job, you're probably better off elsewhere.

• *If you want to know what people think of you . . .* ask them. As part of my application to become a member of the board of directors, I wanted to know how people viewed me as a manager. To find out, I went to people on all levels of our company and asked them to tell me two things I do well, and two things that need improving. I wouldn't let them off the hook until they gave me specifics.

• *Sometimes doing the right thing is not easy.* I almost didn't submit my storybook. I was afraid the directors would think I was crazy, radical, unprofessional. Still, I'm glad I did it, because I'm practicing what I'm preaching and leaders must lead by example.

49

Hurrah for Hollywood

Every once in a while you find something interesting among the bills and junk mail that clutter your mailbox. For example, in early January I found a videotape.

Within seconds of plugging it into my VCR I could tell it hadn't been done by professionals. There was no title. The audio got loud, then soft, for no reason, and the color kept fading. Still, I was curious, and so I kept watching.

The tape introduced a new device that made it simple to replace parts in our radiator traps. The actor removing and installing the Silver Nuggets with the new tool was twelve-year-old Derek Francart. The video's director? Derek's proud father, Armand, who had invented the tool, which is similar to an Allen wrench.

The purpose of the tape was simple. Armand wanted to show that installing and removing Silver Nuggets with this new tool was so easy that even a twelve-year-old could do it.

He had created a wonderful promotion piece to send our sales reps. And in the process, Derek became an Armstrong employee. I sent him his first paycheck ($5) for appearing in the film. I gave his dad a purple ribbon naming him our first creative director of the year. Creativity like his deserved to be rewarded.

If a picture is worth a thousand words, a video may be worth a million. How are you using today's technology to help capture people's attention?

The Moral of the Story

• *Once you have their attention . . .* anything's possible.

• *Creative ideas don't have to be expensive.* Just because it costs more doesn't mean it's better. What did it cost to produce this video? Nowhere near the reported $95 million Hollywood spent to create *Terminator II.* Yet the movie made its point. The new tool would work, and was easy to use.

• *Reward creativity . . .* if you want it practiced. The $5 paycheck, and purple ribbon, told Armand and his son —as well as everyone else who heard this story—that creativity is cherished at Armstrong.

• *Seeing* is *believing.* We could have talked until the cows came home about how easy it was to install and repair Silver Nuggets, but Armand Francart came up with a way that really convinced people.

Thirteen

STORIES TO MAKE EVERYONE A LEADER

50

The Tin Box

Every Thursday, you'll see either the general manager or the controller at Armstrong Machine Works walking around carrying a tin box. What's inside that box? Paychecks. Our paychecks are delivered in person week in, week out to everyone, whether they work in the office or the shop.

Since the general manager or controller is handing out those checks, he must know everybody's name. That's quite a feat when you consider this division has over three hundred people.

Why do we do this? Because we want everybody to have a chance to be heard. While we have an open door policy, not everybody feels comfortable walking into the corner office. By having an officer of the company hand out paychecks, everyone is assured that at least once a week, he'll have a chance to ask a question, voice a concern, or suggest an idea to one of the people in charge.

The secret to success is to do the common things uncommonly well.
—JOHN D. ROCKEFELLER, JR.

The Moral of the Story

• *Show you care.* By handing out paychecks individually, we are—among other things—trying to show that an employee is not just a number. He or she has a name worth remembering.

• *What kinds of questions should our managers be asking when they hand out the paychecks?* Open-ended ones like What can we be doing better? Where do *you* think we can improve? What do *you* think of the new program we just put into place? What one thing would you do tomorrow to make this place more productive? We want people to talk to us, not to respond with one-word answers like yes, or no.

• *Can you walk* and *talk?* Managing by Wandering Around (MBWA), something that we believe in, only works if managers both walk to and talk to the people they see.

• *Are you uncomfortable talking to people?* Don't think you could remember three hundred people's names? It takes practice. But the more you do it, the easier it becomes. Besides, you have to do it. Even if you have an open door policy, not everybody is going to feel comfortable coming to you. If you really want to communicate, you'll have to go to them.

51

Business Is Serious Stuff

"Business is serious stuff" is one of the first things we are taught in school and on the job. But there's no law that says work can't be fun. We hand out cartoons, throw parties to celebrate success, and play jokes on one another constantly. I'm convinced that people work better, longer, and more productively in a place they like. That's why we try to have a little fun at work. Let me tell you three of my favorite stories about that:

What would you say if you received your paycheck in a block of ice? If it had hair glued to it? What if the check was in a helium balloon floating on the ceiling?

"Please don't write a story about this," said Willard Vedmore, in production control, with a smile on his face.

"Why not," I said.

"You'll only give Ken more ideas."

Ken is Ken Clay, financial controller at Armstrong Machine Works, and he's been doing things like this to Willard for many years. It has become a running joke at the division, and everyone can't wait to see what Ken comes up with next. (Personally, I'd like to see this week's check run up the flagpole.) At our company many of the jokes are played between workers and management.

One of the most popular, albeit fattening, jobs at Warrick Controls, in Royal Oak, Michigan, is judging the annual company bake-off. The contest is always held in late January or early February to help people get through the dreary winter.

The competition is fierce. Just about everyone participates. A winner is picked in three categories: hot dishes, cold dishes, and desserts. You receive points on the basis of appearance, taste, and creativity. I remember one entrée was a child's sand bucket filled with a dessert resembling dirt. (It was actually made of white pudding and ground-up Oreo cookies.) You were supposed to eat it with the shovel that was provided. It got my vote for most creative.

The winners receive gift certificates good for a dinner for two. Best of all, when the judging is complete everybody gets to have these delicious foods for lunch.

When someone is getting married, it's customary to give a gift. At AMW we give the potential bride or groom something "symbolic": a ball and chain.

One end of the chain is attached—with a padlock—to the betrothed's leg. On the other end is a weighted ball—ten pounds for men, five for women. You spend the entire day wearing the ball and chain. When the day is finally over, you receive a photograph capturing this tradition.

Imagine trying to do your job while wearing a ball and chain. Imagine the teasing.

Remember to have fun.

The Moral of the Story

• *RELAX!* Informal events like Warrick's bake-off, and traditions like the ball and chain and hiding Willard Vedmore's paycheck, create an atmosphere of fun and relaxation. People talk when they are relaxed and having fun. Listen carefully, you might learn something. ("You" means leaders, supervisors, vendors, salespeople—everyone.)

• *Fun is productive.* There is nothing wrong with taking a moment to play while at work. In fact, we found productivity went up if people took an occasional break. Take your duties seriously, but not to the point where you start burning out.

• *Fun also increases cooperation.* If people enjoy the fellowship of their coworkers, they're more likely to cooperate and work well with them. Good relationships in any company are critical.

• *Good relationships in any company are a must.* These three stories show that Armstrong employees get along very well. The relationship between Ken and Willard allows this type of kidding. Remember, Ken is financial controller, and he is using Willard's paycheck as a joke. Someone's check is pretty sacred. To do what Ken does must mean they are pretty close.

• *The grouch stands alone.* Do your people play well together? The best way I know to determine if people get along is to watch them playing together in a friendly fashion. Do you have someone nobody wants to play with? Odds are this person is also a poor worker because he fails to get along with others. Look for the person no one plays with, when faced with a morale problem. He'll be easy to spot.

52

You Never Get a Second Chance to Make a First Impression

Who's the most important person at your company? The chairman? The chief financial officer? Maybe. But I think you can make a good case for it being the receptionist. After all, the receptionist is often the first person you have contact with at a company. She helps you form a first impression, and the first impression people were getting about us used to be none too good.

People complained that our receptionists were slow to pick up the phone, their tone of voice was too harsh, or they would say things that were inappropriate like "I'm sorry, he's in the men's room" or "He's late coming back from lunch." The customer didn't need to know those things, even if they were true. Sometimes they forgot to say "thank you" or "please hold" and they were not taking detailed messages. In some cases they weren't taking messages at all.

We had our people call our various divisions and found the complaints were justified.

We want every aspect of our company to be professional, so we decided to offer all of our receptionists training.

We took the company plane around the country to pick them up and brought them to the corporate office in Florida. We hired a consultant who specialized in training receptionists, and for several days they worked on their skills.

During the day it was all work, but at night we took them to the finest restaurants, and we made sure they stayed at a nice hotel. We wanted them to know that both they—and this training—were important to us.

It worked. We rarely get complaints about our receptionists anymore. In fact, people are always telling me how wonderful they are.

People judge your company on *everything* imaginable, especially the way you handle phone messages. If you knew a multimillion-dollar order rode on the way you answered the phone, would you change anything?

The Moral of the Story

• *Training must be given* at all *levels of the company.* Few companies train their receptionists. That's too bad. After all, who's more important than the first person who talks to your customer?

• *If you're going to train, and you should, do it right.* That means hiring the best consultants, conducting the meetings at the best facilities, etc. We flew the receptionists to corporate headquarters in the company plane. It was just one more subtle way of showing we were serious about training.

• *Focus on the things that make you unique.* Armstrong is known for quality, so we wanted our receptionists to be known for the quality of service they provided. Quality in this case meant making sure the receptionists were taking accurate, helpful messages and were leaving callers with a positive image of Armstrong.

• *If you want a depressing experience* . . . walk out of the building and down to the nearest pay phone. Call your office and ask to speak to you. You'll be amazed by what happens and what you'll hear.

• *Your receptionist should have a budget.* He should have control over buying things like coffee, rolls, flowers, and umbrellas (so you can offer one to your visitors when it rains).

53

Promises Kept

Buried in the mail one day was a letter from company president Gus Armstrong and his wife, Barbara. On the outside they had written "Promises Kept," and inside was a note hinting at "wonderful things to come."

A few weeks later, Barbara and Gus sent us a photograph of a small sandy island that had one palm tree on it. Again, the message was "promises kept."

Finally, a month later another envelope arrived containing confirmation of what everyone had dreamed about. Our 1991 sales convention would be held in Hawaii.

Since the 1920s, we've had our sales conventions in many wondrous locations: Camel Back, Arizona; Victoria Island, Canada; and Ramuda Ranch in San Diego. But meeting in Hawaii had always been the dream. Back in 1962 Gus said, "One day, we'll get there." And twenty-nine years later, that promise was being kept.

Why this fascination with sales conferences? It's simple. They are the perfect way to:

- Say thank you to our engineers and sales reps.

- Get employees and our sales reps together in a relaxed setting to exchange ideas.

- Discuss new products and new sales techniques.

- Train people.

- Show our independent sales reps how much they mean to us. (The reps are invited, as are all our engineers, salespeople, and managers.) In addition to saying thank you, we are also trying to establish loyalty.

- Motivate the reps to sell our new products.

During the day at our conventions, new products, literature, and services are introduced, and we show the sales staff how the new products work. At night we celebrate and say thank you.

None of this is cheap. On average, our sales conventions cost about 10 percent of our profits in any given year. But it's money well spent. People leave feeling good about Armstrong and their colleagues. And they know how much these things cost, and they don't want to let us down.

They haven't yet. Sales always increase substantially in the year following the convention.

Well done is better than well said.
—BEN FRANKLIN

The Moral of the Story

- *Yes, spouses can come.* First of all, you are asking people to be away from home for about a week, so it's only fair. Second, it gives the "other half" a chance to understand what his or her mate does all day.

• *Do it right.* If you're not going to do it right, don't do it at all. Remember, one of the reasons for holding a convention is to thank people, and there should be no such thing as a cheap thank-you. People need to be motivated to make things happen. Conventions done right motivate them.

• *Invite your independent reps* and vendors who act as partners. It will create greater ties to your company and show that all this talk about "partnership" is really true.

54

Friday Clean-Up Time

We used to stop work thirty minutes before the end of the shift on Fridays so that the factory workers could clean their area. Machines were cleaned of oil, coolant, and shavings and received touch-up paint if they needed it. We'd also use the time to mop, not just sweep, the floor. Over the years, this clean-up time had been cut back to increase production, and because we found some workers took advantage of the tradition. Instead of cleaning their area, they'd go visiting and would wait by the door to leave.

In June of 1990, Armstrong was invited to appear on the "American Spotlight" television show. As part of our appearance, we were told, a camera crew would be coming to our plant. For one solid month before the crew arrived, employees cleaned the factory to ensure it would look good on TV. It had been a long time since this place had looked that nice.

At the production meeting held the day after the TV crew had left, shop foreman Jerry Henry asked that we reinstate the thirty-minute clean-up policy on Fridays. "Let's keep the place looking like it used to," he said. Management agreed. We now make sure people actually clean up during that period, and once again our factory is something we are proud to show off.

Actions speak louder than words. It is not enough to talk about something you'd like done; you have to give people the time and resources to do it.

The Moral of the Story

• *"Here's why we do this."* We must remember to explain to new employees why we do the unusual things we do, so they will understand and practice our culture.

• *Cleanliness is the first step in creating pride.* Pride promotes excellence in everything. Our factory is always clean by anybody's standards. Friday clean-up is like the spring cleaning your house receives. The difference is we do it fifty-two weeks a year, not just once.

• *Cleanliness is a continuous journey.* You never reach your final destination. Jerry Henry understood that; that's why he asked to reinstate the thirty-minute clean-up period on Fridays.

55

Mopping the Shop Floor

During one of my visits to Armstrong's Three Rivers plant in Michigan recently, I had a chance to practice what I preach.

It had been a day where I had been doing all the good stuff: Managing by Wandering Around, Managing by Storying Around, and stressing we had to make decisions NOW! It was 5:45 P.M., and I had a 6:00 P.M. appointment in Kalamazoo. For those of you who don't know it, Kalamazoo is about thirty minutes from Three Rivers. In other words, I was going to be late.

On my way out, I came across a young man in his early twenties who was washing the shop floor. As I was walking by he looked up and said, "Be careful. I just mopped the floor and it's still wet."

I said thank you and kept walking.

On my way out the door I said to myself, "Not bad, David. You actually took the time to say thank you to someone who you'll probably never see again, and he wasn't even an Armstrong employee."

After a few more steps, I realized how dumb I had been.

I walked back to the young man, put my briefcase on the floor, and said, "Excuse me, my name is David Armstrong."

He placed the mop on the floor and stuck out his hand. "I'm Jeff Hudson."

"Jeff, I want to thank you for telling me about the wet floor. I could have fallen down and broken my leg. It's really nice to see someone take so much pride in their work. Thanks again."

By the time I finished, Jeff had a big smile on his face.

"You know," Jeff said, "my boss told me how to do this job. Even though we always put signs up saying 'Wet Floor,' he told me that people never read the signs, and so I should always tell them as they walk by so they won't get hurt."

"Jeff, you're exactly right. I didn't see the sign, let alone read it. Please keep telling our people to be careful."

I was very late for my appointment in Kalamazoo, but darn proud that I was.

If you don't find the time to practice what you preach, you don't believe it.

The Moral of the Story

• *Manage by example.* If you ask people to manage and treat others with respect and dignity, *you* better do it all the time—even if you're running late. It's called integrity.

• *Listen, really listen.* While it's important to give people recognition, that's not enough. Don't give the recognition and then walk away saying, "There, I did my good deed for the day." Take the time, no matter how precious it is, to reinforce the good job. Let people know you mean it.

• *Practice with everybody.* How can you turn your concern for people on and off? Besides, you are a reflection of your company. If you are rude and uncaring to people off the job, the word will get around.

• *People want to be recognized.* And that recognition doesn't have to come in the form of money. Often just hearing "Thanks, you did a good job" is all they want.

56

Go Directly to Jail—and Collect $200

Armstrong Machine Works has several employees who are thrown in jail each year. It always happens the same way. A police car pulls up to the front entrance and the officers lead the employees away in handcuffs.

"But I'm innocent," the employees invariably say. "I didn't do anything."

As with any arrest, the employees soon find themselves in front of a judge. And no matter how much pleading they do, the result is always the same. They're thrown into jail, with bail normally set at $200. The employee is given only an hour or two to raise it.

Fortunately, the events I just described all are designed to benefit the March of Dimes. The police officers are real, but the charges are phony, and the bail money—collected during a series of frantic phone calls to family, friends, and coworkers—is immediately given to the charity.

We're proud of our employees' arrest record.

No good deed ever goes unrewarded.

The Moral of the Story

• *Your reputation stems from many things.* When considering working for a company, people think about the obvious—salary, benefits, possibility for career advancement, and the like—but also the subtle things. Is the company respected? Does it help the local community? Supporting your community is an intangible incentive you can offer your employees, much like a recreation building (we have one) or a fun work environment. It helps create the idea that you are a good company to work for. We work hard at our reputation.

• *Community support works both ways.* Armstrong began when the city of Three Rivers, Michigan gave my great-grandfather a small building and some land in exchange for his promise to employee eight to ten people in our first business—making bicycle spokes. If you support the town in which you do business, the town will support you.

• *Companies like to compare themselves to other companies.* Businesses always measure themselves against their peers. If we support the community, we hope other businesses will see that and decide to do the right thing as well.

Fourteen

STORIES TO
INSPIRE
INNOVATION

57

Mr. Iacocca, Meet Mr. Ghassayi

My favorite Lee Iacocca story involves Chrysler's decision to reintroduce the convertible.

One day while driving around suburban Detroit, Iacocca passed someone in an old Mustang convertible. "That's what Chrysler needs," Iacocca thought. "A convertible."

As soon as he got back to his office, he called the head of engineering. "Well," said the department head, "the normal production cycle is five years. I suppose if we really push, we can have a convertible coming off the line in three years."

"You don't understand," Iacocca said. "I want one to-day! Have someone take one of our new cars to a body shop, have them cut off the roof, and put on a convertible top."

Iacocca had the modified car by the end of the day. He spent the rest of the week driving his "convertible" and found that everyone who saw it loved it. A Chrysler convertible was on the drawing board the following week.

I got to thinking about that story when I heard what Abe

Ghassayi, head engineer at Armstrong-Hunt in Milton, Florida, had done.

Abe had sat through several meetings where we talked about the need to develop a freeze-resistant coil. But for all the talk, nothing had been done.

Abe remembered that when he was a kid, people who owned swimming pools often left a piece of wood floating in them as the weather turned colder. As the water froze, the ice forced the wood out of the pool and filled the space that the wood had occupied. This simple arrangement kept the ice from cracking the pool.

"Why don't we do something similar with our coils?" Abe thought.

Like Iacocca, Abe wanted to move quickly and without spending a lot of money. The problem was it was summer in Florida, and tough to simulate freezing conditions. Abe could have gone to some expensive lab and had it re-create winter, but he realized he didn't have to. "I'll just use the freezer in my home."

Abe went to the factory and picked up two identical coils. He left one as it was and put a rubber eraser, which he hoped would work much like the wood did in swimming pools, inside the other. He then filled them with water, welded the ends shut, put them both inside the freezer, and went to bed.

In the morning, Abe found the coil without the eraser had ruptured, while the one with the eraser had not.

We were on our way to having a freeze-resistant coil.

"Perfectionism is spelled p-a-r-a-l-y-s-i-s."
—WINSTON CHURCHILL

The Moral of the Story

• *Think cheap.* Almost always there's an expensive way and an inexpensive way to try something. And almost always the inexpensive way gives you a faster answer, as Abe proved by putting the coils in his freezer.

• *It doesn't have to be perfect.* Would we have rushed into production with a freeze-resistant coil based just on Abe's experiment? No. But he proved the idea had merit. Prototypes don't have to be perfect; all they have to do is show that the idea *looks* feasible.

• *Failures can be good, too.* Abe's idea worked. But even if it hadn't we would have learned a lot—quickly and without spending a fortune.

• *Innovation is like baseball.* The more tries at bat, the more hits. The more ideas you try, the more successes you'll have.

58

Small Starts

Abe Ghassayi and Lynn Snider have never met, but they have a lot in common.

We were having a problem manufacturing the fish finders produced by Computrol. The ratchet rings were out of tolerance and would fit only if forced. To make sure they'd stay in place, you had to place a socket over the ratchet ring and then hit it with a rubber mallet. Not only was this cumbersome, it was dangerous. It wasn't helping our quality either.

Lynn Snider at Computrol saw the problem as an opportunity. On his own time—and using $5 of his own money to buy some cardboard and lumber, plus odds and ends found in his garage—he developed a press that would install the rings safely and efficiently.

Lynn's ratchet press wasn't perfect, of course, and we've modified it over the years (for example, we now use an air cylinder to press on the rings), but Lynn's resourcefulness went a long way toward solving the problem.

Every product goes through a failure phase. The only question is when. Better early than later.

The Moral of the Story

• *Small starts are the best starts.* We call what Lynn did a small start, an inexpensive, simple attempt at solving a problem. Once a small start proves effective, we spend the money to take the idea further.

• *Small starts are cheaper.* Always.

• *Small starts are easier to accomplish.* And if you get a "win" right away, you're motivated to immediately begin work on the next phase.

• *Small starts are easier to kill.* If you don't have a lot of time or money involved, you're usually not reluctant to stop working on an idea. The more money involved, the less likely people are to concede defeat, because they are afraid of writing off the investment.

• *Everyone counts.* People like Lynn and Abe, and the countless others at our company who innovate on their own time, using their own money, continue to make our company strong and prosperous. Everyone can make a difference, if she believes she can.

• *Spread the word.* Let people know you want them to be resourceful. Tell stories about people who show initiative; promote them; hand out a $5 bill for a good effort *that doesn't work.* People will respond.

59

Don't Reinvent the Wheel

Implicit in Abe's story is our basic management philosophy. We try not to overcomplicate things. We don't want to keep reinventing the wheel. The creation of our new line of humidifiers is a case in point.

The Electronic Humidifier Unit (EHU) 500 is based on old technology, but is great for hotel chains or large office buildings, any place where you need to humidify a *large* area. The EHU 600 is built using newer technology that efficiently humidifies *small* areas such as doctors' offices, dentists' waiting rooms, and small businesses.

To take care of the demand for a more efficient large-area humidifier, we could have come up with a third technology, but Kevin Foran, an application engineer, had a better idea. He told Eric Kruger, who works assembling humidifiers, to take the electronic components out of an EHU 600 and put them inside a gutted EHU 500. That was our starting point, and we continued to modify the hybrid unit until we had a humidifier, containing all the features our customers requested, that could cover a large area efficiently. David Fischer, product engineer, performed product testing that confirmed that the new humidifier met our safety and quality standards. We now offer three entirely different kinds of humidifiers.

Simpler is better.

The Moral of the Story

• *Why waste time?* Why spend time or money developing new approaches to solving a problem? When faced with something new, your first question should always be, "What do we have in-house that can be adapted to take care of this?"

• *Use that R&D money elsewhere.* Take the money you would have spent trying to reinvent the wheel and apply it to improving your manufacturing process.

• *Two (or three or four or . . .) heads are better than one* in developing new products, as Kevin, David, and Eric proved in creating a new humidifier. That's especially true if you are trying to adapt an old product to a new use. Everyone—sales, marketing, accounting, engineering, manufacturing, purchasing—should be working on the adaptation.

60

K.I.S.S.

Thomas Edison had a unique way of hiring new engineers. He'd give the applicant a light bulb and ask, "How much water will it hold?"

There were two ways to find the answer. The first choice was to use gauges to measure all the angles of the bulb. (That's not easy, given the shape of a light bulb.) Then with the measurements in hand, the engineer would calculate the surface area. This approach could take as long as twenty minutes.

The second choice was to fill the bulb with water and then pour the contents into a measuring cup. Total elapsed time: about a minute.

Engineers who took the first route, and performed their measurements by the book, were thanked politely for their time and sent on their way. If you took the second route, you heard Edison say, "You're hired."

Why guess when you can try?

The Moral of the Story

• *Try it, you (just may) like it.* Theories, assumptions, and guesses are seldom accurate. Actually trying something is quicker, more accurate, and much more fun.

• But always remember: K.I.S.S.—keep it simple, stupid.

• *Turn the "conventional wisdom" upside down.* One way that's almost always guaranteed to produce a creative solution is to ask what the "conventional way" of solving the problem is. Then do the opposite.

• *Looking to hire creative people?* Develop an Edison test of your own.

61

We're Shameless Thieves

As children we're taught stealing is wrong. But in business, that's not always true. You should "borrow" unpatented ideas from the best people and companies you can find. It's an efficient way of satisfying your customers, and we do it all the time. Case in point, Fish D'Tect, made by our Computrol division.

A couple of years ago there were a lot of fish finders on the market, but they all had one major problem. They couldn't tell you if the object they had found hidden beneath the water was a stone, log, or fish.

Then Humminbird, one of our major competitors, came out with a fish finder that showed little red squares on the screen when the object below was probably a fish.

We thought that was a good idea, so we borrowed it—and improved it. Instead of squares, we showed fish shapes. We also showed the size of the fish. Either a small, medium, or large fish appears on the screen, depending on the size of the fish in the water. This new feature has helped Computrol gain market share.

When it comes to new ideas, we are shameless thieves.

The "if it's not invented here we won't use it" syndrome can be fatal. There's nothing wrong with swiping an unpatented idea if the idea will help you do a better job serving your customers.

The Moral of the Story

• *Steal with pride.* Use any unpatented idea, no matter what the source, if it will help you do a better job of taking care of your customers. Don't be embarrassed that you are borrowing ideas. Be proud of the fact that you are doing everything you can to take care of your customers.

• *Looking for ideas to steal?* Look to the best. You want to study how the leaders in their field do things.

• *Don't just steal—improve.* Appropriating the idea is not enough. Make it better. Tailor it to fit your customers' exact needs. We took those little red squares and replaced them with fish.

• *Stealing is everybody's job.* While we expect our salesmen and engineers to practice "creative swiping," looking for new ideas is something everyone should be encouraged to do. Send employees to other departments (and to your competitors, if you can) to see how they do things.

62

Drilling Holes

Herb Johnson, quality assurance manager at Armstrong Machine Works, has "a thing" about scrap. He hates to see us junk a part because it was manufactured badly. He's not alone. Every single manager is proud that our scrap rate is just 0.2 percent. To make sure that we remain as efficient as possible, "scrap" is always an item on the agenda at the production staff meeting held every Thursday.

It was at one of those staff meetings, not that long ago, that Herb started to get upset.

"You know what I found yesterday in the scrap bin?" he asked. "A casting with three times too many holes drilled in it. How could a machinist have made such a mistake?"

Doug Criswell, the foreman in the machine department, was happy to explain.

"Our new machines allow us to set up the alignment by computer, but, Herb, as you know, you can't do that with our older machines. So the first piece that we run through one of our older machines is usually a test piece, where we check the alignment and the size of the holes," Doug said.

"But instead of throwing that piece away after the test is

completed, we decided to use it again and again and again, as the test piece for setting up another machine. That's why you saw so many holes."

Herb was very happy, and the meeting continued.

Innovations can be nothing more than doing an old task a new—and more efficient—way. Teach an old dog a new trick.

The Moral of the Story

• *Everyone can innovate.* You don't need a new products department to come up with new products. Everyone should have the power to develop—*and implement*—new ideas. That's exactly what the people in our machine department did.

• *Share the word.* An innovation that is never implemented is worthless. An innovation that is not shared is not worth much more. Talk up your new ideas with your colleagues, or post the idea on a bulletin board. Heck, you can even tell a story about it.

• *Waste not, want not.* What are you throwing out? How can it be: (a) saved, (b) reused, (c) put to another use, or (d) recycled? The payback will be faster, and a sure thing. Look for innovations that will save you money as well as lead to new products.

Fifteen

STORIES TO GET PEOPLE TO COMMUNICATE ABOUT THINGS WORTH COMMUNICATING ABOUT

63

The Flasher

Much to the surprise of the people at Computrol, Bill Bogan wanted to add an obsolete feature to the division's new fish finder.

Bogan, the sales manager, knew Computrol's strategy for gaining market share is based on always providing the newest, most advanced product on the market. But still, he wanted to add a "flasher mode" to our new fish finders. Computer circuits, which allowed us to identify not only a fish but also its probable size, had made the flashers outdated. Who, after all, would want a device that simply flashed when a fish was nearby, when you could have a fish finder that indicated the fish's location and size?

Some of our longtime customers, that's who, Bogan said. "Some of our older fishermen are not ready to make the change to the more technical fish finders," he said. "They're uncomfortable with high tech. They want a simple-to-read fish finder."

Nobody agreed with Bill, but he was persistent and finally convinced everyone to add the flasher. Customers tell us it is one of their favorite features, and we are selling many units because it's there.

If you want to know what people want, ask them—and listen to what they have to say.

The Moral of the Story

• *Listen, listen, listen.* If you can't spend time with your customers directly—and for the life of me, I can't figure out why you can't—listen to your salespeople. They're in touch with your customers daily. Your customers and salespeople know what's needed. Don't second-guess them.

• *Is this feature necessary?* Technology is a wonderful thing, but just because you've come up with the latest gizmo doesn't mean customers are going to want it. Debit cards, electric cars, and VCRs based on Beta technology all worked just fine. The problem was customers didn't like any of them.

• *Everything old is new again.* One way to differentiate yourself from the competition is to bring back an old feature or an old way of doing things. Old Coke was a smash when they brought it back.

64

Perception Is All that Counts

"Listen, Armstrong-Hunt, you're wrong," the customer yelled. "I don't care what your records show, you're wrong."

We weren't, but if the customer thinks you're wrong, you're wrong—even if you're not.

That message was brought home again to me recently when we filled an order for a customer who wanted coils that were to be cut at a specific angle.

We delivered the coils, prepared just as the customer had specified, but he called up to complain.

"We ordered the fittings at a thirty-eight-degree angle," the customer said. "You sent us fittings at forty-one degrees. We need these fittings fixed now!"

David Boykin, plant manager at Armstrong-Hunt, called the sales department and asked, "Did we send the right fittings?"

A clerk pulled the order and said, "Yes, sir. it says forty-one degrees in black and white."

Nonetheless, David sent several people out to the customer's plant to reweld all the fittings. The customer was happy. For a moment.

When the customer went to install the coils, he called again. "These coils are too heavy."

David checked again and found the coils were exactly to spec, but the customer had never dealt with this type of coil before and so was unprepared for its weight. Even though we had done everything right, David had two of his men—Doug Randolph, shop lead man, and Bill Patterson, welder, stay an extra day at the customer's plant so they could design a tool that would help him install the coils.

What started off as a difficult situation—after all, the customer had been complaining—ended quite well. Not only did the customer write a thank-you letter to David Boykin, he tried to hire Doug and Bill. (They turned him down.) We're expecting another large order from this customer shortly.

Perception is all that counts.

The Moral of the Story

• *Perception is all that counts.* The customer perceived the coils to be wrong, even though the coils met the original specifications. Without arguing, we fixed the problem—*quickly.*

• *Perception is all that counts.* The customer's perception was the coils were too heavy and difficult to install. That perception stemmed from his inexperience with the coils. Nevertheless, we helped him design a tool that would make it easier for him to do the installation.

• *Perception is all that counts.* Have we made the point?

65

Is the Grass Always Greener?

What do you do when you have full-time employees and a job that can be done only half the year?

That's exactly the problem we face in doing our steam trap surveys.

As a service to our customers, we periodically check to see if their traps—which might have been installed by us, or by one of our competitors—are operating at 100 percent efficiency. If they're not, we tell the customers and they're replaced.

The problem is the survey can be done only during the six months of the year when it's cold and the plants are using steam. That means in winter we are extremely busy, but in summer there is virtually nothing to do. We pride ourselves on not laying off people, which precludes us from hiring people during the busy season and then letting them go when things get slow.

In 1982, we figured out a solution to our problem. The manufacturing and office people would be trained to do the surveys. During training seminars, we explain to them how the traps work, what they should look for during the survey, and how to use the testing equipment. Plus we teach them the etiquette of dealing with customers.

The idea of cross-training has worked out so well that we now use it elsewhere in the company. For example, Mary-anne Undrosky, who works as a receptionist at Everlasting Valve, has been trained so that she can fill in as a sales-woman. Once when her division was desperately trying to hit its sales quota, she managed to sell $35,000 in boiler valves in two weeks *during her spare time.*

To meet increased competition, you have to be flexible. Cross-training gives you that flexibility.

Everybody's job—even the boss's—gets boring sometimes. What could be better than allowing people to switch off every once in a while? You'll end the boredom, and the employee who moves (temporarily) into the new job will gain a different perspective.

The Moral of the Story

• *Cross-train. Cross-train. Cross-train.* It doesn't neces-sarily mean having a person on machine A learning how to run machine B. It can mean having a secretary be a sales-person, or putting an accountant out in the field to do surveys. This flexibility will help lower your costs and make it easier to compete.

• *You want your people to stay close to your customer, right?* What better way to do that than sending them out into the field, especially if they spend the bulk of their time behind a desk or operating a machine. They'll get immedi-ate feedback about what they have to do to take care of their customers.

• *Maybe the grass* isn't always *greener* on the other side. How many times have we heard people say they wished they had somebody else's job? By sending our office and shop people on the road—especially to call on clients overseas—they discover maybe they don't have it so bad after all. Eating out night after night after night, staying in hotels for long stretches at a time, and traveling on a plane for twenty-two hours is not all it's cracked up to be.

66

Y CN'T U RD THIS?

Marcelle Ory ne fait pas partie du personnel d'Armstrong S.A. Elle est employée par les Ets Laurenty, une société de nettoyage de la région. Depuis qu'elle a commencé à nettoyer les bureaux d'Armstrong, il y a une dizaine d'années, elle s'est indentifiée d'une façon telle à Armstrong S.A. que chacun imagine qu'elle fait partie du personnel de la Société.

Roger Closset, Directeur Général d'Armstrong S.A., disait: 'c'est incroyable de trouver quelqu'un comme Marcelle, si fière de son nettoyage. Nettoyer signifie vraiment quelque chose pour elle. Elle accomplit son travail comme une vraie professionnelle et avec passion. Elle se soucie du moindre détail et rien n'échappe à sa vigilance. On l'appele parfois 'Sherlock Holmes.' Grâce à ce trait de caractère, nous avons évité bien de problèmes après les heures de fermeture de l'usine."

Marcelle travaille de 16h30 à 21h00. Elle s'intéresse à tout. On lui a appris comment remplacer le papier du fax, de surveiller l'ordinateur après les heures de travail (si un problème surgit, elle appelle un responsable à son domicile).

Si l'on oublie d'éteindre sa machine, elle le fait, etc. Récemment, un groupe important de 15 visiteurs italiens devait venir au laboratoire pour un séminarie. Bien que cela ne fut pas de son ressort, Marcelle accomplit un travail formidable pour que la laboratoire fut prêt à temps, car le laboratoire avait été laissé sale et dans un désordre complet, par le personnel qui s'était occupé des modifications de l'installation. Ce personnel n'était pas au courant de la visite des Italiens. Quand Marcelle a vu le laboratoire dans cet état déplorable, elle l'a nettoyé de fond en comble, travaillant tard le soir.

Grâce à l'intérêt porté par Marcelle, une situation embarrassante a été évitée.

Marcelle est fière de son travail. Lorsque l'on ne fait pas attention et que l'on crée du désordre, elle se fâche et demande à la personne concernée, peu Importe qui, de faire attention.

Parlez-vous français?

The Moral of the Story

• *You can't read this?* Why not? Doesn't everyone read French? A true international company tailors its products and literature to the needs of the country it is doing business in. Speaking and writing the customer's language is a sign of courtesy and respect. It also makes it easier to communicate clearly with the public.

• *Learn the way* they *do things, too.* In Japan, business cards are handed out with both hands, one at a time. The card should face the receiver, so that it's easy to read. After you hand out the cards, you bow. In America, we hand out business cards as if we're dealing cards. Learn the customs so you won't inadvertently offend anyone.

• *One last thought.* Don't forget to use their paper standards. Most countries use longer sheets of paper than we do in America. Will your binders hold their size of paper?

67

Small Words, Active Verbs

I bet you had the same eighth grade English teacher I did. She had you read *The Catcher in the Rye* and *A Separate Peace,* explained the difference between similes and metaphors until you thought you would pass out from boredom, and always gave you the same advice when it came to writing: Never use the same word twice in the same paragraph, and, above all, never use a small word when a big one will do.

I don't know why they taught us that. Maybe the idea was to get us used to looking up words in the thesaurus. Whatever the reason, people started using three-, four-, and five-syllable words, and it quickly got to the point where nobody—me included—knew what they were talking about. A lot of people still talk that way.

I have a bad vocabulary, and I'm proud of it.

I can talk to anyone, and he will understand me.

I talk slowly, using simple words, the kind I'd use with my nine-year-old son.

Just about everyone I know has a bigger vocabulary than I. That's great. For some people, using big words is a hobby. But everyone's education is not the same. By using the shortest, simplest words I know, I'm sure I'm communicating—and isn't that why we talk?

Circumlocution obfuscates.
Translation: Big words confuse people. Speak simply.

The Moral of the Story

• *Are you communicating?* Showing off your vocabulary is only going to confuse people.

• *Do you want an easy standard to follow?* Ask yourself, would a ten-year-old understand what I'm saying? Is using language like this patronizing? Not if you talk to everyone this way.

• *No initials.* Be careful not to use abbreviations. Not everyone knows what MBO (Management by Objective) or ROE (Return on Equity) means. If you use the abbreviation, also explain it, at least the first time.

• *Speak up.* If they don't hear you, you are not communicating.

Sixteen

STORIES ABOUT
WHY SMALL
IS BEAUTIFUL

68

Red, White, and Blue

The American flag is an important symbol, but recently I saw we weren't giving it the respect it deserved.

I noticed as I walked around outside our office that the flag flying in front of our building was frayed at the edges and the colors looked faded. I immediately informed our outside maintenance people about the problem. They replaced the flag the same day. Once again, the red, white, and blue is flying proudly in the wind.

There are no "little things."

The Moral of the Story

• *Little things mean a lot.* We must be aware of *everything* that might give the perception of poor quality or service. If we don't take care of our country's most valuable symbol, our customers might legitimately ask if we care about quality, service, or anything else.

• *Congratulations, you've just been named Ambassador.* Everyone can make a difference. Consider yourself ambassador of the company, no matter how small the detail.

• *Correct the problem now.* If you find a problem—big or small—try to fix it immediately. There is no excuse for not trying. Any delay can be seen—and rightly so—as a lack of caring.

69

The Throne

What would you do if the most popular chair in your company were broken? If it were the boss's chair, would you fix it right away? If it were your chair, would you fix it right away?

How about if it were an employee's chair?

One day a secretary in our Everlasting Valve division walked up to controller Dick Base and said, "Dick, the toilet seat in the ladies' restroom is very loose."

"I'll get it fixed right away," Dick said, and following proper procedures, he called the maintenance crew and asked them to take care of it.

Two weeks later:

"You know, Dick, the seat still isn't fixed."

Dick couldn't believe it. He *immediately* went down to the engineering department to get some tools. Then he walked over to the ladies' restroom. After knocking to make sure it was empty, he entered, and while still wearing his three-piece suit, got down on his hands and knees and fixed the seat. He was going to make sure that the problem was fixed today! And thanks to Dick, it was.

Are we, as leaders, here to be served or to serve?

The Moral of the Story

• *Leading by example sends a powerful message.* I'm sure every manager at Everlasting Valve now realizes just how important taking care of your people really is. Having your division's controller fix a toilet seat, while wearing a three-piece suit, sends this message loud and clear.

• *Creating a sense of* urgency *in everything is vital.* By putting his work aside and immediately going to fix the seat, Dick gave everyone an example of what it means to "take action now." Dick did not put it off until the next day because he had too much work to do or because he was wearing a nice suit. He took care of the problem right then.

• *Leaders listen.* Paying attention and active listening (really listening) are key traits of successful leaders. Dick listened to the secretary's complaint and really cared. Understand, this was in the ladies' restroom. The toilet seat really didn't matter very much to him personally, since he uses the men's room. But Dick cares about his people. He paid attention, listened, and fixed the problem. No problem is too small to fix.

70

Lites

I got a copy of a letter than a salesman had sent to his supplier (us), and at first I was pleased. "Things are going well in replacing the defective part on you're product," the salesman wrote. "But I've noticed that the indicator lights are burned out on 25 percent of the models."

When I looked into it, it was even worse. The failure was *at least* 25 percent. And this defect had been present since day one, and the product had been on the market for more than ten years.

"Why hasn't anything been done about this?" I asked.

"We have had other problems with the product that were more serious," I was told.

Don't they understand, I said to myself. What could send a louder message of poor quality than burned out indicator lites on the front of our product? Our customers see these burned-out lights every day; that's a daily reminder of our poor quality. What is more serious than that? Our reputation is being damaged—daily.

The fact noboidy is interested or willing to do anything about this shows they think some things are too small to be bothered with. But to a customer, that isn't the case. Customers perceive any problem—big or small—as something that should be fixed.

When it comes to quality, *nothing* is too small to be ignored.

The Moral of the Story

• *U probably found several mistakes in this story.* And even if you said to yourself, "What's one page out of several hundred?" I bet it still bothered you. Have I made my point? Little things *do* matter.

• *Little failures can lead to big failures.* Don't overlook something, even if it appears to be of little significance. You never know how someone is going to judge you.

• *To a customer, there is no such thing as a small problem.* If the customer has a problem—no matter how minor it may seem to you—you can guarantee that it is a big deal to him. Treat it that way.

Seventeen
STORIES ABOUT
FINDING NEW
SOURCES OF
PROFIT

71

Hidden Assets: Your Retirees

One of the oldest clichés in the book is "out of sight, out of mind," but I found out recently just how true that old saying is.

We were having a great year. Sales were climbing, and the increased orders, coupled with a shrinking work force due to retirement, were making it extremely hard for Armstrong Machine Works to ship products on time.

There were several meetings called to figure out what to do, and out of the many options available—making overtime mandatory, hiring new workers, etc.—we finally realized there was a much more efficient answer.

Grant Kain, plant manager, said to his secretary: "Etta [Griffin], would you pull the list of the people who recently retired?"

She does. Grant stares at the first name on the list and picks up the phone.

Grant: "Bill, this is Grant at Armstrong. Would you be interested in coming back to work for a while?"

Bill: "Grant, how much time are we talking about?"

Grant: "Bill, we will take as much as you can give us, but

no more than thirteen weeks so that we don't jeopardize your Social Security benefits."

Bill: "When do you want me to start?"

Asking some of our retirees if they could come back and help us out until the crunch was over was one of the smartest things we ever did. The response from our retirees was overwhelming, and the quality and productivity of their work was outstanding.

It was the perfect solution. The retirees got a chance to see old friends and make a little extra money. (Most worked between ten and thirteen weeks, the maximum amount of time they could be employed without jeopardizing their Social Security checks.) They gave up (for a little while) the retirement that they had worked so hard for, to assist the company they loved.

Their company was grateful. People in the shop—and in the front office—welcomed them back. They knew the retirees would do a better job than a trainee. And we also knew using the retirees on a part-time basis would help us prevent overstaffing.

Everybody benefited, and you can bet that the experience our retirees have to offer will never be "out of mind" again, even though they might be out of sight.

Your best new employee is often a retired employee.

The Moral of the Story

• *Your chances of hiring success are greater* . . . if you hire a retired worker. No matter how good your interviewing process is, you never know for sure if someone will work out. But in rehiring retirees, you only have to invite back your most productive workers, and you already know who they are. The retired worker requires little training.

She can immediately go to work and be productive. It takes us six months of training before a new hire's work is up to our standards, and six months is too long to wait.

• *I'm flexible, you're flexible, and everyone's secure.* Armstrong wants to provide job security, but it's extremely difficult to do. By bringing back retired employees as needed, we can avoid hiring new full-time workers. We can remain lean.

• *It's the right thing to do.* A worker's relationship with a company shouldn't end once she retires. Offering the retiree her old job back shows her we still care.

• *You're also increasing your ROI.* You spent a lot of time and money training the worker who recently retired. By inviting her back, you're getting a nice return on that investment.

72

Forty-five Years of Service

After forty-five years of service, and very few sick days, we were going to lose an ideal worker. A retirement party was scheduled for Friday afternoon.

Forty-five years of doing the same job without a complaint.

Forty-five years of hard work, *every day of the week*.

Forty-five years of dedication deserved to be rewarded.

That vintage 1945 air compressor was sure going to be missed.

Why throw a party for a machine? Jerry Gilchrist, assistant general manager of Armstrong Machine Works, explained, "We got forty-five years of service out of this compressor. Money well spent, don't you think? That's something to celebrate."

I'm sure that through the decades, people thought about replacing the compressor with a newer, fancier model. But they never did, because the old machine got the job done.

We must be careful not to always purchase the newest

piece of machinery on the market. If the machines and tools we have are doing the job, there's just no need to replace them. Many of the machines we have are from the 1950s, but they work just fine. We're number one in our industry, and we provide the best quality in the market. We don't need the newest machinery to be competitive. We don't need the newest machinery to be innovative.

Let's appreciate our old machinery and recognize it for what it is—a good investment.

Just because it's new doesn't mean it's better.

The Moral of the Story

• *So you never buy new equipment?* Of course we do. But there has to be an overwhelming reason. Once word processors and personal computers came along, it was silly to keep using typewriters. But there must be a compelling reason before we buy something.

• *What's a compelling reason?* Calculating pay-back periods—that is, trying to figure out how long it will take for the new piece of equipment to pay for itself—is silly. First, those projections are only estimates. Second, you can rig the numbers any way you want. Third, many times the justification given for the purchase is not implemented. For example, "if we buy this machine, we can reduce the work force by two people." The machine is bought, but the people stay. Either you desperately need the new thing or you don't.

• *How will you know, for sure?* The easiest way is to put the person who will be using the new device in charge of buying it. Once you do, you can be sure she'll research every competing brand on the market, and be thoroughly convinced it's needed, before spending the money to buy it. She won't play games with the pay-back period because she knows her credibility is on the line. If she says it's needed, it's probably needed.

13

Space: The Final Frontier

(Music swells. Then a basso profundo voice, coming from the center of an echo chamber, is heard.)

Announcer: Space. The final frontier. This is the story of Armstrong. Its ninety-two-year mission to store anything of useless value. Come with us now as we boldly go where we've never been before. To the basement.

. . .

We were running out of space, and people were talking about the need for a new warehouse, and maybe even another office building. I wasn't against the idea, providing we actually needed the space, but I wasn't sure we did.

I decided to find out. I began by looking in our basement, where I knew we had office equipment dating back to the 1950s, and more than a hundred file cabinets. As I went through the folders, I found corporate tax returns dating back to the 1920s, a copy of every payroll check ever issued, and invoices that were thirty years old. I asked executive secretary Jeanette Whitney to supervise a crew who would clean out the basement. By the time they were done, 50 percent of the basement was empty.

I then started going through our various departments. There were folding chairs, covered with dust, leaning against walls, and prototypes for ideas we had long since abandoned could be found all over the place.

I spent two full days doing nothing but going from department to department convincing people to purge useless junk. Sometime in the past management had sent the message that they should save everything, either in their offices or in a warehouse. I had to convince people that was no longer true.

Jerry Gilchrist, assistant general manager, came up with a wonderful way of getting that message across. "If we disagree on the value of something, why don't we tell people that they have to keep in their office one item that they want to store? When someone has to give up space in his own office, it helps clarify the importance of the item he thought he 'had to' save."

The mission was a success. By the end of the second day, we had found enough space to keep all departments happy.

Space is too valuable a resource to waste.

The Moral of the Story

- *Is this worth the CEO's time?* Aren't there more important things for the head of the company to do than go around cleaning out closets? Well, my "housecleaning" kept us from building a $200,000 warehouse. There are very few things I can do in forty-eight hours that can save the company this much money.

- *When in doubt, throw it out.* A good rule of thumb is: If you haven't used it in a year, it's probably not worth keeping. Throw it out, or if it's worth more than $500, sell it.

• *Continuous cleaning.* While we solved our space problem in two days, we'll be up to our eyeballs in junk again in five or ten years unless it's clear to everyone why we have to continually get rid of useless stuff.

• *Trap the rats.* At work, most people are pack rats. Self-interest ("I may need this again someday" or "It took me a long time to develop this, I'm not going to throw it away") is a strong motivation when it comes to keeping junk. We must learn to look beyond our department's needs to see the needs of the entire company. It was well known that Armstrong required more space, and the price of that space would be an expensive new building. The question everyone had to ask was: Is my department's junk really worth that expense?

74

The Golden Weed Award

One of the things I found as we went on our quest to find more space was that in every office, the credenzas and desks were bulging with files, and almost all the filing cabinets were filled and overflowing. New filing cabinets always were in demand. We were always short of manila folders. Filing took too long, and there was always someone at the copy machine. It was clear we had no paper retention policy.

The unwritten policy at most companies is to keep a copy of anything you write or receive. If you ask why, you hear things like: "This is valuable information that I might need one day"; "My boss may ask for a copy"; "Let's keep it just in case"; or even "It's a matter of CYA."

But the cost of making copies, sending copies through the mail, reading them, and filing them (not to mention the space they take up) makes this policy extremely expensive. And the irony is we seldom look again at all those papers once we've filed them.

The main reason people hesitate to dispose of copies is their worry about possible legal ramifications. And we were no different. Most employees didn't know how long documents had to be kept. Tom Morris, our general counsel, decided to solve the problem.

He boiled the hundreds of pages of record retention laws and guidelines down to two pages and sent his summary to every department head. Tom suggested that anything we didn't need to legally keep, or that we didn't look at often, should either be shredded or burned. (We want to make sure confidential information doesn't end up in the hands of a competitor.) Tom later presented a videotape that made the same points.

A year later, he went further. He suggested that each department periodically have a "weeding party" to dispose of documents that had outlasted their usefulness. Whoever does the best job of weeding now receives the "Golden Weed Award" and dinner for two.

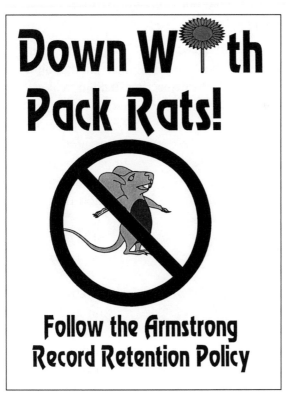

Want an easy way to cut down on unnecessary memos, reports, and letters? Turn down all requests to purchase new filing cabinets.

The Moral of the Story

- *People always complain they don't have enough time* . . . yet they are reading and making copies, filing them, and sending them out "FYI." All this takes time, time that should be spent on more urgent projects.

- *Here's an easy way to save money.* Don't make copies. The cost of reading, copying, and creating files is expensive. Do it as a last resort.

- *Think about what might happen.* If people stopped sending copies to each other, they might use the phone more and start meeting face-to-face. Who knows what might happen if there were two-way communication?

75

The $1.2-Million Maintenance Man

Walter Deacon, senior applications engineer, had agreed to move into a new office, but he just hadn't had time to move. Jerry Gilchrist took care of that in a hurry.

One day when Walter was out of town on a business trip, Jerry went to everyone in the sales department and convinced them it would be fun to surprise Walter by moving him into his new place while he was gone.

One by one the salespeople fell in love with the idea, and in a matter of moments, you had the entire sales staff grabbing chairs and bookcases and moving Walter's stuff into its new home. They even rehung his pictures and watered his plants.

Later, plant manager Grant Kain stopped by Jerry's office and said, "Jerry, it's been a long time since I've seen any of the office people move their own furniture. It's about time they did. Congratulations. I've always wondered why maintenance had to move a desk, change a light bulb, or carry a fold-up chair down the hall."

I know, I know. You're much too busy to move your own furniture or change your own light bulbs. But are you too busy to save $1.2 million? That's what a $30,000-a-year maintenance man is going to cost your company during the forty years he's likely to be with your firm. If you look at it that way, can't you water your own plants?

The Moral of the Story

- *Why can't we move our own furniture?* Somewhere in the past, we as leaders must have set an example that said anything that had to be moved should be moved by the maintenance department. How foolish. Why couldn't the office people move their own furniture? There are several strong men in the department who could help move heavy furniture.

- *Practice what you preach.* Shortly after Jerry set the example, I helped move a heavy table from one end of the building to the other. Of course we took the long way to ensure that everyone noticed David Armstrong moving furniture. If the boss can do it, everyone can do it.

- *Even if you're the president . . .* you can move furniture. Titles do not give us the right to think we are too good to help out around the office. Think of it this way: By helping move furniture, you save the company $1.2 million, the lifetime cost of adding a maintenance worker. That's worth *anyone's* time.

- *Common sense will prevail.* Will ninety-eight-pound weaklings (male or female) try to carry a desk by themselves? No. They'll ask for help. There goes the workman's comp reason for not moving your own furniture.

76

Good Things Come in Small Packages

Caroline Rentfrow, who works part-time in the accounting department, found a problem with Armstrong Machine Works' water and sewage bill. It looked much too high. The bill that had been $900 a quarter was now $3,400.

After double-checking to see that there hadn't been a rate increase, Caroline took the matter to Harriett Romig, AMW's head of accounts payable, who called the city, which said the bill was correct.

City officials went on to remind Harriett how the bill is calculated. The city assumes that water which goes into a company comes back out through the sewer lines. So it takes the water charge and doubles it to cover sewage usage.

But as Caroline and Harriett pointed out, the city was forgetting one thing. Years ago, we had shown that water used for our sprinkler systems, and in the heat treatment department, did not come out through the sewer lines. It was recycled. The city previously had even put meters on the sprinklers and in the heat treatment department which proved that was the case. Still, as a look at the bill showed, the city, for some time, had been taking the water charge for those two departments and doubling it, just as if the water were coming back out through the sewage lines. We found that we had been overcharged by $18,867 since 1985. The city reimbursed us.

With size comes waste, no matter what you do. The best you can hope for is to keep the waste to a minimum.

The Moral of the Story

• *Correcting a thousand little things is far better than correcting one big thing.* One thousand times $18,867 equals $18,867,000. What big thing could we do to save that much money?

• *Sew up those deep pockets.* Armstrong is getting big, and it is easy to think the company has deep pockets. People may think a few dollars here or there won't matter. "Send it Federal Express. It's only $12. Armstrong can afford it." This is one way companies get into financial trouble. Before you send something by overnight mail, why don't you call to see if the person is going to be there?

• *You don't have to pay a bonus if employees save you money.* First of all, coming up with good ideas—which are often money-saving ideas—is part of their job. Second, how do you decide who should get a bonus? If someone saves the company more than $1,000? $5,000? How much would you give her? And no matter what you do, there is bound to be jealousy. ("How come she got a bonus for her idea, and I didn't get one for mine?") We congratulated Harriett and Caroline for a job well done and told them both this is exactly the kind of thing that gets people promoted.

Eighteen

STORIES ABOUT HOW TO TELL STORIES

77

Glimpses into the Future

It's the year 2000 and, as always, I'm practicing Management by Storying Around. Suddenly all my stories start coming back to haunt me.

- "David, you talk about *fast failure* being okay, as long as we learn from it. Well, I just had someone make a $50,000 mistake. That's okay, isn't it?"

- "David, you talk about fairness, yet Armstrong Machine Works has a sick leave policy which pays you to stay well, a production bonus, and a recreation building. Why don't we have those things at our division?"

- "David, now you've done it. A competitor just 'creatively swiped' one of *our* products. They bought your book, took your advice, and used it against us."

Storytelling makes you *really* think through the way you do things and what you believe.

I do want people to make mistakes. If you aren't willing to fail, then you aren't willing to do anything. And as long as people learn from their mistakes and keep the risk to a manageable size, I think mistakes are fine.

If we have a policy, I want it to be defensible. Yes, AMW has a lot of benefits, chosen by its employees, but so do our other units. At Armstrong-Hunt, they've opted to work ten-hour days, four days a week, so they always can have a three-day weekend.

And if a story we tell helps a competitor, so be it. A better competitor forces us to be better. (Besides, what I really think will happen is our competitors will read our stories and become frustrated because they can't do business the way we do.)

Only write stories you want practiced. You'll be forced to live by what you write.

The Moral of the Story

• *If storytelling does nothing else . . .* it will allow you to have a friendly employee manual that shows new hires how you do things and what the company believes.

• *Storytelling can create jealousy.* People will read about the perks and benefits in your other divisions and wonder why they are not equally blessed. Once the stories are distributed, be prepared to explain—in detail—why you do the things you do. One possible explanation is that each division is unique and should be treated that way.

• *Storytelling puts you in charge.* You get to play author. You have control over what topics are included and what morals should be stressed. By taking a glimpse into the future, you can avoid many potential problems.

• *Will stories help your competitors?* Maybe. But better competition makes us better.

78

A Story
About Storytelling

For years, I had wanted to hire Rex Cheskaty, an engineer at Grumman Aircraft, but I couldn't get him to even look at Armstrong. I knew he had a great future at Grumman. He had already been employee of the year—twice—had led the creation of several key projects, and was being seriously considered for a high-level management slot. Still, periodically I'd visit him—he lives nearby—to see if he were interested in joining us.

Finally, I got a break—thanks to storytelling.

"Rex, Doubleday/Currency wants to publish my stories about Armstrong," I said during one of those visits. "I want to make sure that the stories have value to a person who works at another company. Would you take the time to read them and tell me if you learned anything from them, or how I could make them better?"

Less than a month later, Rex called back.

"David, are these stories true?"

"Yes, or they wouldn't have any meaning."

"David, I can't believe these stories are true. You make it sound as if Armstrong is the ideal company for anybody."

"Well, the easiest way to find out is to visit Three Rivers and check us out."

Rex did. And I am happy to say he's now our director of engineering.

We use the stories in other ways, too.

When we were interviewing potential engineers, I handed the battery story to one prospect and asked him what he got out of it. I had thought this person was too rigid and too negative to fit into our company, and his analysis of the story confirmed it.

"You don't have the right systems," he told me after reading the story. "If you did, people wouldn't have been taking the batteries for personal use in the first place and Ken Clay would have known what was going on before he got the expense voucher."

"But what about the part about needless bureaucracy?" I asked.

"Just a minor point," he said. "As the story makes clear, the problem is really with your systems."

We didn't hire him.

It's a fine thing to have ability, but the ability to discover ability in others is the true test.

The Moral of the Story

• *Storytelling can be used for recruiting.* I had tried everything I could think of to entice Rex to join Armstrong. The stories convinced him.

• *Storytelling can help during your job interviews.* If your stories are sincere and show the direction you want your company to take, they can be a valuable interviewing tool. After an applicant reads a story—or stories—and tells what he agrees or disagrees with, you'll know if he truly believes in your philosophy. Pick the right story for the right person. If you're interviewing an engineer who'll be designing new products, pick a story about innovation. If a person is interviewing for management, pick a story on leadership. You may want the prospect to read several different stories to get an idea of how he would work with departments other than his own.

• *Have the interviewee tell you a story.* If the person you're thinking about hiring can't tell you a good story about where he works, odds are he's done nothing outstanding in his current job. If he does tell you a story, listen to how he does it. Is it told with sarcasm? Humor? Sincerity? Detailed facts? Imagination? This can tell you as much about the person as the story itself.

79

How to Write a Story

What follows is the detailed checklist I use to write my stories. I hope you find it helpful when you write yours.

THE BASICS

1. Always begin with a heroic deed.
2. The story must be true. Verify all facts.
3. Think of a clever title. (It helps capture the readers' attention.)
4. Stick to one idea or theme.
5. Keep the story short. No longer than one single-spaced typed page.
6. People like to see their names in print. Use their names.
7. Use words that form a mental picture. Keep your words folksy; the story should read just as you tell it. It's more entertaining that way.

WHEN AND HOW YOU TELL STORIES

1. Tell a story when there is a specific point you want to make.

2. Make sure the story is distributed to everyone. Either send everyone a copy or post the story on the bulletin boards.

3. Always frame the original and give it to the person—or persons—mentioned in the story. It's a form of recognition.

POTENTIAL PROBLEMS

1. It is going to take time to find the heroic deeds to write about.

2. If you leave out someone's name, you'll hurt his feelings.

3. You may not get all the facts rights. Total accuracy is impossible. Do the best you can.

BENEFITS (THERE ARE A LOT)

1. You are giving recognition of heroic deeds.

2. You are reinforcing your corporate vision.

3. Storytelling helps the company stay focused.

4. The corporate culture becomes widespread.

5. Stories are friendly, therefore you are fostering communication.

6. You're forced to go and talk to people to find potential stories, which gets you involved in all areas of the company, which, of course, is a primary objective of MBSA —managing by storying around.

7. Storytelling provides training, it shows people what's expected of them.

80

Write Your Own Story Here

Here's a chance for you to write a story of your own. (A suggested outline is shown below.) When you're finished tell someone the story. Start with your friends, and then try it on people in the company you don't know as well. Remember to have fun. Good luck.

Title
(Make it catchy, teasing, enticing)

FACTS:

MENTAL IMAGES:

Don't forget to include a quote box. It helps break up the text, and it gives you another chance to underscore the point you want to make in the story.

Write your story here. Be creative and imaginative.

Keep the story short and single-spaced. Does it fit on this page?

The Moral (Try to have Three) of the Story Goes Here:
(The first line should make your point. Put it in boldface.)

•

•

•

I would love to hear how you put storytelling to work at your company. Please send me your favorite story: David M. Armstrong, Armstrong International Inc., 2081 E. Ocean Blvd., Stuart, Fla. 34996.